Modern Myths Series

Horror

by

Marcus Grant

HEINEMANN EDUCATIONAL BOOKS

LONDON

Heinemann Educational Books Ltd
LONDON EDINBURGH MELBOURNE AUCKLAND TORONTO
HONG KONG SINGAPORE KUALA LUMPUR
IBADAN NAIROBI LUSAKA
JOHANNESBURG NEW DELHI

ISBN 0 435 10350 4

Published by
Heinemann Educational Books Ltd
48 Charles Street, London W1X 8AH
Filmset in Photon Univers 12 pt. by
Richard Clay (The Chaucer Press), Ltd, Bungay, Suffolk
and printed in Great Britain by
Fletcher & Son, Ltd, Norwich

Contents

Acknowledgements

The author and publisher wish to thank the following for supplying the illustrations.

The British Film Institute: II:A, II:D, II:G, II:H, II:K, II:L, III:A, III:H, III:J, III:K, IV:F, IV:G, V:B
Cambridge University Library: II:B, II:F, II:J, III:B, III:M, IV:D, IV:K, VI:A, VII:A, IX:A (copyright *The New Yorker*)
Radio Times Hulton Picture Library: III:E
Edinburgh City Libraries: III:C, III:D
Warren Publishing Co: II:C
Marvel Comics Group (*The Incredible Hulk* Vol 1, no. 133) II:E
Midi Minuit Fantastique (January 1963): IV:C, IV:H, IV:J, IX:B
The New Statesman: VIII:A

Preface

This book is in two main sections. The first (I–V) contains the text, which includes explanatory and critical comment together with extracts from original source material. The books from which the extracts have been selected are all (with the possible exception of Egremont's *Bride of Frankenstein*) easily available and part of the purpose of this section is to encourage students to read the complete books. The main purpose is, however, to present the origins and principle developments of the myths and to indicate the central issues which they raise.

The second section of the book (VI–IX) contains suggestions for discussions, written work and various kinds of projects related to the myths examined in the first section. It should be emphasized that these questions and projects are not intended to be exhaustive but rather to suggest the range of possibilities which can be developed in the work of individuals and groups. There is also a separate discussion of the advantages and particular problems of using film and VTR equipment as an educational tool in this area.

The pictorial material in this book is intended to form an integral part of its structure and not to be merely illustrative. This is primarily a workbook rather than an anthology.

When I wrote this book, I was lecturing in English and Liberal Studies at Cambridgeshire College of Arts and Technology. I would like to thank all my colleagues who helped me in so many ways, and in particular Sydney Bolt, Henry Merritt and Keith Crook. I also received valuable advice on general and particular matters from Richard Allen, Johnny Owens, Paul Moffat, John Harvey, Roy Park, Andy Anderson and Annie Grant. Most of the research involved in compiling this book was undertaken at Cambridge University Library and at the British Film Institute.

I Introduction

1   The stories of the characters you are going to read about in this book are all what could be called *modern myths*. None of the stories in this book even existed before about 1800, which makes them, as myths go, very modern indeed. The origins of the characters in the stories may be either real or fictional. What makes them modern myths is that they have appeared in some particularly powerful popular form and this has persisted so that now they can be instantly recognized by almost everybody. We accept the stories as if they were true, although in the form we have them we know quite well that they must be either semi-fictional or totally imaginary. We use the names of these characters quite frequently in ordinary conversation and we expect people to understand what we are talking about. The stories must contain some special kind of meaning for us, which may be hidden but is highly relevant to how we live today.

2   The modern myths in this book are all of one general kind. They are all *horror monsters*. There are many other horror monsters in books and in films which may be extremely frightening but which are not modern myths. The choice of which monsters are most important is to some extent a personal one, but you must bear in mind the general characteristics of modern myths. The stories in this book are familiar, at least by name, to most people and they also suggest areas of meaning which extend beyond the stories. They are also more or less frightening.

3   It is precisely because we are so familiar with these stories that it is worth looking at them in a rather more objective way. The relationship of a myth to the society which produces, develops and nourishes it is a highly complex one. A myth is a kind of metaphor for some of the values which underlie that society. In examining these modern myths, what we are doing is examining modern society and the particular forceful images which it projects of itself. Since modern society means us, what we are really doing is finding out about ourselves.

4   There is something which we call everyday life or normal existence, which might be described as *reality*. And there is something different from this, proceeding from the imagination, which might be described as *fantasy*. There is, however, no clear-cut distinction between these two states. What myths do is to inhabit the overlap between reality and fantasy. They are obviously *not true*, yet they obviously *express truths*. The quality of any society can often usefully be seen by reference to the structure of its active myths. That being so, it is worth considering, as you read the stories in this book, what exactly it means in relation to our own society that Frankenstein, Jekyll and Hyde, and Dracula should exert the particular influence they do.

II Frankenstein

1   The first thing to realize about *Frankenstein* is that the name refers not to the monster but to the man who created the monster. The monster has no name and is originally referred to simply as "the monster" or occasionally "the demon". The confusion about the name has probably arisen because the films on this theme always use the word *Frankenstein* in their titles, and yet it is the image of the monster which people remember. The result is the mistaken assumption that it is the monster who is called Frankenstein.

2   Mary Shelley, the wife of the poet Shelley, was only nineteen years old when she wrote *Frankenstein*. She and her husband were on holiday in Switzerland in the summer of 1816. The weather was particularly bad and it had rained non-stop for several days. There happened to be a book of German ghost stories in the house, and Lord Byron, who was a friend of theirs and lived near by, suggested that they should each write a ghost story of their own. Byron himself began a story called *The Vampyre*, but the only one actually to be finished at the time was Mary Shelley's *Frankenstein*.

3   At first she had difficulty trying to think of a suitable story: "one", as she said, "which would speak to the mysterious fears of our nature, and awaken thrilling horror – one to make the reader dread to look round, to curdle the blood, and quicken the beatings of the heart". The idea came to her suddenly one night after she had gone to bed particularly late. Earlier that day she had overheard her husband and Lord Byron discussing the experiments of Dr Erasmus Darwin, who was rumoured to have preserved artificially a piece of dead worm until it came back to life and began to move of its own accord. There was also, at the beginning of the nineteenth century, great interest in the new science of *galvanism*, which was to do with the use of electrical energy to stimulate activity in living things. The founder of this science, Galvani, originally noticed the legs of dead frogs twitching when an electrical charge was applied to them.

4   Thus, the idea of man creating life artificially already seemed a possibility when Mary Shelley wrote *Frankenstein*. At that time, of course, the scientist was a more unfamiliar and suspicious figure than he is now. The story plays upon our fear of the unknown. The scientist is shown tampering with the laws of nature. Even though science has become better understood and the figure of the scientist more familiar, we are still aware of the dangers in going too far. Today this is clearly seen in the growing anxiety about what terrible effects pollution is having on the world we live in. Meanwhile, the possibility of man creating life has become a probability. With test-tube babies and spare-part

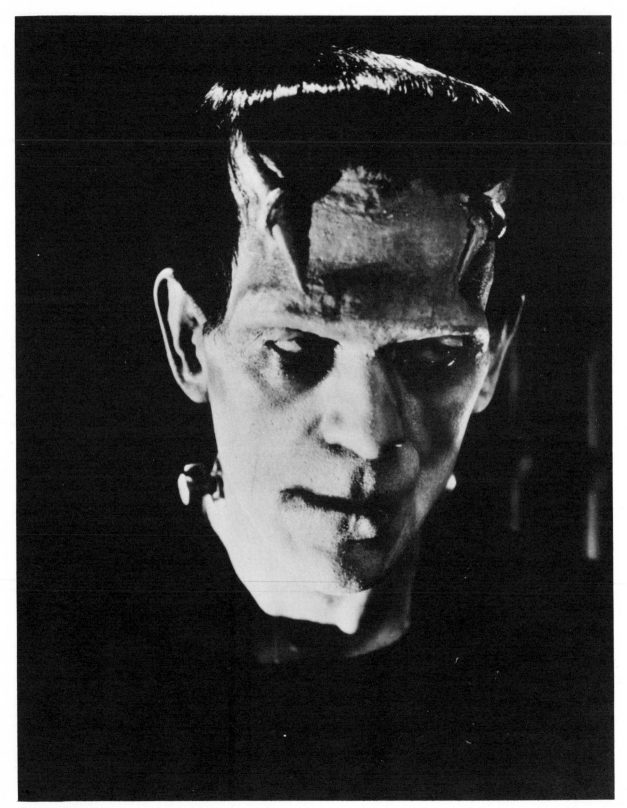

surgery, the myth of Frankenstein is just around the corner from what is actually happening in laboratories now.

5   Mary Shelley's story is presented by a narrator who is on a voyage of discovery to the North Pole when he picks up a well-educated stranger who has been marooned on an ice-floe. The stranger is Victor Frankenstein, who eventually tells the narrator the story of his life. He explains how he went to Geneva University and became passionately interested in the problem of the origin of life, how suddenly he discovered the solution to that problem and how he went on to create a living creature. The monster Frankenstein makes is an example of what is known as the *noble savage* — that is to say, he does no evil until he comes into contact with the injustices of society. He wants to be loved, but is met everywhere by hatred because he looks so hideous. The rejected love turns into hate and destructiveness; his greatest desire is to revenge himself upon Frankenstein for having created him. He murders Frankenstein's youngest brother William, his best friend Clerval, his bride Elizabeth and in fact almost everybody who is in any way close to him. The book ends with Frankenstein pursuing the monster for weeks across the polar ice-cap, only to be murdered by him in the cabin of the narrator's ship.

6   *Frankenstein* is one of the most famous horror stories in the world. It also marks the beginning of *science fiction* as a distinct kind of writing. Yet in Mary Shelley's original story, it is surprising how little science and even how little horror is actually present. About Frankenstein's experiments, the descriptions, though lurid enough, are particularly vague.

(a)   I pursued my undertaking with unremitting ardour. My cheek had grown pale with study, and my person had become emaciated with confinement. Sometimes, on the very brink of certainty, I failed; yet still I clung to the hope which the next day or the next hour might realise. One secret which I alone possessed was the hope to which I had dedicated myself; and the moon gazed on my midnight labours, while, with unrelaxed and breathless eagerness, I pursued nature to her hiding-places. Who shall conceive the horrors of my secret toil, as I dabbled among the unhallowed damps of the grave, or tortured the living animal to animate the lifeless clay? My limbs now tremble and my eyes swim with the remembrance; but then a resistless, and almost frantic, impulse urged me forward; I seemed to have lost all soul or sensation but for this one pursuit. It was indeed but a passing trance that only made me feel with renewed acuteness so soon as, the unnatural stimulus ceasing to operate, I had returned to my old habits. I collected bones from charnel-houses; and disturbed, with profane fingers, the tremendous secrets of the human frame. In a solitary chamber, or rather cell, at the top of the house, and separated from all the other apartments by a gallery and staircase, I kept my workshop of filthy creation: my eye-balls were starting from their sockets in attending to the details of my employment. The dissecting room and the slaughter-house furnished many of my materials; and often did my human nature turn with loathing from my occupation, whilst, still urged on by an eagerness which perpetually increased, I brought my work near to a conclusion.

II : A. *Boris Karloff as Franken-stein's monster.*

5

7   Obviously the reader does not expect full do-it-yourself instructions for every stage of Frankenstein's activities. In fact, we are given almost no details at all about what exactly is going on. The science is a mystery.

(b)   It was on a dreary night of November that I beheld the accomplishment of my toils. With an anxiety that almost amounted to agony, I collected the instruments of life around me, that I might infuse a spark of being into the lifeless thing that lay at my feet. It was already one in the morning; the rain pattered dismally against the panes, and my candle was nearly burnt out, when, by the glimmer of the half-extinguished light, I saw the dull yellow eye of the creature open; it breathed hard, and a convulsive motion agitated its limbs.

How can I describe my emotions at this catastrophe, or how delineate the wretch whom with such infinite pains and care I had endeavoured to form? His limbs were in proportion, and I had selected his features as beautiful. Beautiful! – Great God! His yellow skin scarcely covered the work of muscles and arteries beneath; his hair was of a lustrous black, and flowing; his teeth of a pearly whiteness; but these luxuriances only formed a more horrid contrast with his watery eyes, that seemed almost of the same colour as the dun white sockets in which they were set, his shrivelled complexion and straight black lips.

The different accidents of life are not so changeable as the feelings of human nature. I had worked hard for nearly two years, for the sole purpose of infusing life into an inanimate body. For this I had deprived myself of rest and health. I had desired it with an ardour that far exceeded moderation; but now that I had finished, the beauty of the dream vanished, and breathless horror and disgust filled my heart. Unable to endure the aspect of the being I had created, I rushed out of the room, and continued a long time traversing my bedchamber, unable to compose my mind to sleep. At length lassitude succeeded to the tumult I had before endured; and I threw myself on the bed in my clothes, endeavouring to seek a few moments of forgetfulness.

But it was in vain: I slept, indeed, but I was disturbed by the wildest dreams. I thought I saw Elizabeth, in the bloom of health, walking in the streets of Ingolstadt. Delighted and surprised, I embraced her; but as I imprinted the first kiss on her lips, they became livid with the hue of death; her features appeared to change, and I thought that I held the corpse of my dead mother in my arms; a shroud enveloped her form, and I saw the grave-worms crawling in the folds of the flannel.

I started from my sleep with horror; a cold dew covered my forehead, my teeth chattered, and every limb became convulsed: when, by the dim and yellow light of the moon, as it forced its way through the window shutters, I beheld the wretch – the miserable monster whom I had created. He held up the curtain of the bed; and his eyes, if eyes they may be called, were fixed on me. His jaws opened, and he muttered some inarticulate sounds, while a grin wrinkled his cheeks. He might have spoken, but I did not hear; one hand was stretched out, seemingly to detain me, but I escaped, and rushed down stairs. I took refuge in the courtyard belonging to the house which I inhabited; where I remained during the rest of the night, walking up and down in the greatest agitation, listening attentively, catching and fearing each sound as if it were to an-

II : B. *The first picture of Franken-stein and the monster. This engrav-ing by W. Chevalier is the frontis-piece to the 1831 edition. It shows Frankenstein rushing from his labor-atory as the monster (in foreground) shows the first signs of life.*

FRANKENSTEIN.

"By the glimmer of the half-extinguished light, I saw the dull, yellow eye of the creature open; it breathed hard, and a convulsive motion agitated its limbs. ... I rushed out of the room."

Page 43.

London; Published by H. Colburn and R. Bentley, 1831.

nounce the approach of the demoniacal corpse to which I had so miserably given life.

Oh! no mortal could support the horror of that countenance. A mummy again endued with animation could not be so hideous as that wretch. I had gazed on him while unfinished; he was ugly then; but when those muscles and joints were rendered capable of motion, it became a thing such as even Dante could not have conceived.

7

8   It is not *how* the monster is created that matters; just that he *is* created. The story of *Frankenstein* begins from the belief that a man can create life artificially. The details you must provide, if you want to, from your own imagination. The same is largely true of the horror. There are scenes which rely for their effect on a build-up of suspense, but there are hardly an descriptions which are in themselves horrible or frightening. Even the description of the monster coming to life (*b*) only becomes horrible because we are seeing him through Frankenstein's eyes. The monster, in any case, only *looks* horrible. Certainly at first, he is gentle and innocent, wanting only to love and be loved. But the book is written as if Frankenstein was telling the story to us. This means we can share his feeling of horror at having created the monster. But we can also stand further back from the action than he can and feel pity for the monster, which he never does.

9   Here is an extract from the monster's own account of his first few days of life. Notice the difference between this and the way Frankenstein talked in the previous two extracts. The monster is reasonable and does not get carried away with emotion. He is a sympathetic figure, confused, frightened and looking for help.

(*c*)   It was dark when I awoke; I felt cold also, and half-frightened, as it were instinctively, finding myself so desolate. Before I had quitted your apartment, on a sensation of cold, I had covered myself with some clothes; but these were insufficient to secure me from the dews of night. I was a poor, helpless, miserable wretch; I knew, and could distinguish, nothing; but feeling pain invade me on all sides, I sat down and wept.

It was about seven in the morning, and I longed to obtain food and shelter; at length I perceived a small hut, on a rising ground, which had doubtless been built for the convenience of some shepherd. This was a new sight to me; and I examined the structure with great curiosity. Finding the door open, I entered. An old man sat in it, near a fire, over which he was preparing his breakfast. He turned on hearing a noise; and, perceiving me, shrieked loudly, and, quitting the hut, ran across the fields with a speed of which his debilitated form hardly appeared capable. His appearance, different from any I had ever before seen, and his flight, somewhat surprised me. But I was enchanted by the appearance of the hut: here the snow and rain could not penetrate; the ground was dry; and it presented to me then as exquisite and divine a retreat as Pandaemonium appeared to the daemons of hell after their sufferings in the lake of fire. I greedily devoured the remnants of the shepherd's breakfast, which consisted of bread, cheese, milk, and wine; the latter, however, I did not like. Then, overcome by fatigue, I lay down among some straw, and fell asleep.

It was noon when I awoke; and, allured by the warmth of the sun, which shone brightly on the white ground, I determined to recommence my travels; and, depositing the remains of the peasant's breakfast in a wallet I found, I proceeded across the fields for several hours, until at sunset I arrived at a village. How miraculous did this appear! the huts, the neater cottages, and stately houses, engaged

II : C. *Advertisement in a modern American Horror Comic.*

II : D. *First film monster: Charles Ogle in a publicity still for the 1910* Frankenstein.

II : E. *Two frames from an American* Hulk *comic. Compare this with the scene described in paragraph II. See also paragraph 17.*

my admiration by turns. The vegetables in the gardens, the milk and cheese that I saw placed at the windows of some of the cottages, allured my appetite. One of the best of these I entered; but I had hardly placed my foot within the door, before the children shrieked, and one of the women fainted. The whole village was roused; some fled, some attacked me, until, grievously bruised by stones and many other kinds of missile weapons, I escaped to the open country.

10   The first *Frankenstein* film, already with what was to become an obligatory happy ending, was a black and white silent made in 1910 with the monster played by Charles Ogle. By far the most famous screen version is, however, James Whale's *Frankenstein* filmed in 1931 with Boris Karloff as the monster. This was also shot in black and white, but many of the prints were tinted a particularly lurid green. Apart from the happy ending and numerous omissions, the most important departure which the film makes from the original book is that the monster is given a madman's brain by mistake. Instead of the innocent creature driven to murder by the cruelty of society, the monster of the film is a murderous fiend, virtually incapable of speech and almost totally lacking in reason.

11   The only scene in which our sympathy for the monster is really

aroused is when, lost and filled with blind hatred, he comes across a little girl by a lakeside. Instead of running away from him, she asks him to play with her and together they throw flowers into the water and watch them float. Expecting her to float like the flowers, the monster picks up the little girl and throws her in amongst them, where she drowns. The film ends, not at the North Pole, but with the monster apparently burned to death in a windmill.

12   Three years later appeared *The Bride of Frankenstein*, the first of many sequels. In fact the idea of creating a mate for the monster is already present in Mary Shelley's original story, although there Frankenstein repents before the work is complete.

(*d*)   I trembled, and my heart failed within me; when, on looking up, I saw, by the light of the moon, the daemon at the casement. A ghastly grin wrinkled his lips as he gazed on me, where I sat fulfilling the task which he had allotted to me. Yes, he had followed me in my travels; he had loitered in forests, hid himself in caves, or taken refuge in wide and desert heaths; and he now came to mark my progress, and claim the fulfilment of my promise.

As I looked on him, his countenance expressed the utmost extent of malice and treachery. I thought with a sensation of madness on my promise of creating another like to him, and trembling with passion, tore to pieces the thing on which I was engaged. The wretch saw me destroy the creature on whose future existence he depended for happiness, and, with a howl of devilish despair and revenge, withdrew.

13   In *The Bride of Frankenstein*, the monster (still played by Boris Karloff) rises from the smouldering ruins of the windmill to spread death and terror over the countryside. The monster is befriended by a blind hermit, only to be forced to flee again as soon as he is discovered by somebody who can see. Hiding in the vaults beneath a cemetery, he meets Dr Pretorius, a particularly nasty example of the mad scientist type, who happens, like Frankenstein, to have succeeded in creating living beings. The only trouble is that his specimens never grow to more than four inches in height. Pretorius visits Frankenstein (who has, for some reason, changed his name from Victor to Henry for this film) and tells him about his limited success.

(*e*)   The old Doctor pursed his thin lips, as he bent his piercing gaze on his young companion.

"You think I'm mad," he muttered. "Well," ignoring Henry's gesture of dissent; "perhaps I am . . . But listen, Henry Frankenstein. While you were digging in your graves, snatching limb and bone and sinew from the cadavers there; piecing the dead tissues together, and welding the dead flesh into a monstrous lampoon of the living; I, my dear pupil, went for *my* materials to the very source of life. . . ."

Henry stared, only half comprehending what the other was saying. "You mean . . ."

"I mean that I grew my creatures like cultures: grew them as Nature does – from seed."

II : F. *A grave-robbing scene from Reynold's* Mysteries of London. *Before the science of anatomy was made legal, the only way to obtain bodies was to steal them from recent graves. Edinburgh's Burke and Hare are the most famous example of the trade. Sometimes they anticipated the natural death of their victims in order to save themselves the trouble of digging.*

Henry had sunk down into a chair, his elbows resting on the table, his chin cupped in his hands. He said: "After this, you must tell me why they made you leave the University. I heard things, you know . . . But, one doesn't always give credence to tales; and the tales were very wild. . . ."

"Yes, I shall be pleased to tell you. It was nothing infamous. Only . . . well – only a little *unusual*, say."

Henry said: "Tell me more of these cultures of yours."

"Oh, yes, the cultures . . . Yes, as I said, I grew them as Nature does – from seed. I studied the growth of the human body: not from birth, but from the very moment when the female seed is fertilized in the mother's body. Many years I spent in research; for anatomical dissection is unfortunately not yet included in the curriculum of our medical schools, and my practical work was not too easy to come by.

"Still, I managed somehow to learn what I wanted. And then, when not only each stage in existence was clear in my mind, but more, the *reasons* why each stage should and must succeed the preceding one, then, and then only, did I begin my great experiment – the artificial germination of the human protoplasm."

14 That last extract was from Michael Egremont's *novelization* (a novel written from the screenplay) of *The Bride of Frankenstein*. The story goes on to tell how Dr Pretorius persuades Frankenstein to collaborate with him in making the mate for the monster. He overcomes Frankenstein's reluctance by kidnapping his bride Elizabeth. They eventually succeed in giving life to the she-monster, only to discover that she, like everyone else, finds her intended mate repulsive and horrible. Frankenstein just manages to escape with Elizabeth from the laboratory before the monster blows it up, killing Dr Pretorius, the she-monster and himself.

15 In this second extract from Egremont's novelization, Dr Pretorius and Frankenstein have just succeeded in bringing the she-monster to life. Notice how different the monster appears here from Mary Shelley's picture of him.

(*f*) And as they unwound the cerement-like wrappings, so their wonder grew.

For the flesh that lay revealed beneath, the smooth firm contours of a young girl's face, was flushed with the bloom of youthful health.

"She is . . . beautiful," the Doctor whispered after a while.

"Yes . . . she is beautiful . . . !"

Above that small face, with its wide, staring eyes, the hair grew strangely straight and long. It radiated fan-wise from her brow, like some outlandish head-dress, and on the left side, a white streak showed vividly against the raven black of the rest.

"Faulty pigmentation again," the Doctor muttered.

But Henry said nothing: he was too rapt in the contemplation of this lovely alien thing.

So immersed were they, indeed, that they did not hear the door open behind them, and a gaunt shape, as horrible as this was lovely, pad silently into the room.

They were only aware of the intrusion as, in hateful, familiar tones, the cry: "Friend . . . !" fell upon their startled ears, and the eyes before them filled with emotion for the first time; the emotion of *fear*. . . .

Pretorius and Henry turned round to confront the Monster; but his regard was not for them.

Grinning foolishly, he stumbled towards the seated girl, his hands working spasmodically, with the pleasurable excitement that was filling him.

"Friend . . ." he mouthed, drooling with obscene desire, ". . . friend . . . !"

And now life came swift and sudden to the seated figure. The grinning face was very near her own, when she screamed. Stridently: frenziedly. Screamed again, and again, and again; until with a gasp, she fell forward, and Henry caught her in his arms.

Tenderly he bore her to the sofa and laid her down. The Monster came ambling behind him, hands and eyes twitching with nervous excitement.

He put out a hand to caress the recumbent girl: but the Doctor pulled him roughly aside.

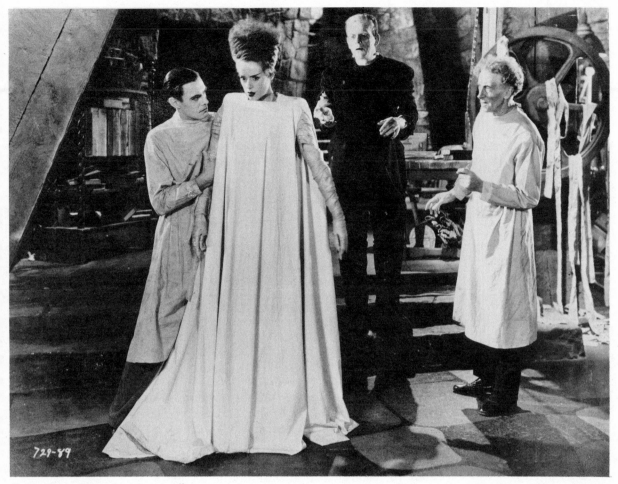

II : H. *The She-monster recoils from the monster.*

II : G. *Elsa Lanchester as the She-monster in* The Bride of Frankenstein.

"Stand back!" he snarled.

The Monster paid no attention. He brushed the Doctor aside, and sat down on the sofa, taking the girl's hand and fondling it with clumsy endearments.

"Oh God! Henry, what *are* we to do?"

He turned angrily to the Monster.

"Stand back, you!"

Henry whispered:

"Wait . . ."

The girl was beginning now to recover. An eyelid flickered, and her breathing became regular. The Monster was still chafing her hand.

Her eyes opened, and she saw the dreadful face beside her.

Her hand drew back in terror.

"Wait . . ." said Henry.

The Monster put his paw on her white thigh; stroking the soft, smooth skin.

"Friend. . . ."

There was a scream: this time almost more penetrating than before. The girl jumped up from the sofa, and ran to Henry.

He put his arms about her, contemptuous of the Monster's snarls.

"Listen, Pretorius, I'm taking her downstairs. I'll wrap her up, and give her some food." He looked disdainfully at the Monster, as he added, "See if you can't keep this *thing* quiet!"

As the door closed behind them, the Monster growled:

"She hates me . . . like others. . . ."

"No . . . no," the Doctor said soothingly. "She is tired."

The Monster seemed to consider that. He blinked suspiciously at the Doctor, then gazed uncertainly at the closed door.

He shook his head.

"No . . ." he said deliberately, "she hates me . . . like others. . . ."

And then a slow, evil smile passed across that white scarred face: and seeing it, the Doctor's soul sickened within him.

The Monster nodded.

"You make , , , her?" pointing with a long, dirty finger at the other.

"Yes!" Pretorius whispered, through dry lips.

The Monster nodded.

"Then . . . she . . . belongs . . . me?" he leered, and turned towards the door.

Perhaps, in that awful moment, Dr Pretorius found his sanity. Perhaps, as the Monster moved off, he realized what a terrible price one must pay when one tampers with those things that a Divine Wisdom has bidden us to leave alone.

In one sickening flash of understanding, he realized that what had been created a slave, was now their master. That the destiny of all of them was in the hands, and at the whim, of this ungainly, uncomely, half-witted brute.

16   In the story of *Frankenstein*, there are three basic characters: the creator, the monster and the victim. You can see the whole story as an exploration of the relationships between these three characters. If the monster murders because it knows no better, is it the monster's fault? Or is it the fault of the creator for having made the monster in the first place? Or is it even the victim's fault for failing to understand the monster?

17   The victim must be shown as completely innocent in order to appear as vulnerable as possible. That is why children are such clear favourites when it comes to finding suitable victims, closely followed by defenceless young ladies. The more helpless the victim, the greater your thrill of fear in the face of the monster's potency. The monster frightens you because he is *alien*, that is to say unnatural, and therefore something you believe you cannot understand. At the same time, it frightens you simply because it is so strong and cruel. Here, from each book, is a scene in which the monster confronts a helpless victim. In the first extract, which is from Mary Shelley, Frankenstein has just married Elizabeth and they have crossed Lake Como to be alone on the first night of their honeymoon.

(*g*)   It was eight o'clock when we landed; we walked for a short time on the shore enjoying the transitory light, and then retired to the inn and contemplated the lovely scene of waters, woods, and mountains, obscured in darkness, yet still displaying their black outlines.

The wind, which had fallen in the south, now rose with great violence in the west. The moon had reached her summit in the heavens and was beginning to descend; the clouds swept across it swifter than the flight of the vulture and dimmed her rays, while the lake reflected the scene of the busy heavens, rendered still busier by the restless waves that were beginning to rise. Suddenly a heavy storm of rain descended.

I had been calm during the day; but so soon as night obscured the shapes of objects, a thousand fears arose in my mind. I was anxious and watchful, while my right hand grasped a pistol which was hidden in my bosom; every sound terrified me; but I resolved that I would sell my life dearly, and not shrink from the conflict until my own life, or that of my adversary, was extinguished.

Elizabeth observed my agitation for some time in timid and fearful silence; but there was something in my glance which communicated terror to her, and trembling she asked, "What is it that agitates you, my dear Victor? What is it you fear?"

"Oh! peace, peace, my love," replied I; "this night and all will be safe: but this night is dreadful, very dreadful."

I passed an hour in this state of mind, when suddenly I reflected how fearful the combat which I momentarily expected would be to my wife, and I earnestly entreated her to retire, resolving not to join her until I had obtained some knowledge as to the situation of my enemy.

She left me, and I continued some time walking up and down the passages of the house, and inspecting every corner that might afford a retreat to my adversary. But I discovered no trace of him, and was beginning to conjecture that some fortunate chance had intervened to prevent the execution of his menaces, when suddenly I heard a shrill and dreadful scream. It came from the room into which Elizabeth had retired. As I heard it, the whole truth rushed into my mind, my arms dropped, the motion of every muscle and fibre was suspended; I could feel the blood trickling in my veins and tingling in the extremities of my limbs. This state lasted but for an instant; the scream was repeated, and I rushed into the room.

Great God! why did I not then expire! Why am I here to relate the destruction of the best hope and the purest creature of earth? She was there, lifeless and inanimate, thrown across the bed, her head hanging down, and her pale and distorted features half covered by her hair. Everywhere I turn I see the same figure – her bloodless arms and relaxed form flung by the murderer on its bridal bier. Could I behold this and live? Alas! life is obstinate and clings closest where it is most hated. For a moment only did I lose recollection; I fell senseless on the ground.

When I recovered, I found myself surrounded by the people of the inn; their countenances expressed a breathless terror; but the horror of others appeared only as a mockery, a shadow of the feelings that oppressed me. I escaped from them to the room where lay the body of Elizabeth, my love, my wife, so lately living, so dear, so worthy. She had been moved from the posture in which I had first beheld her; and now, as she lay, her head upon her arm, and a handkerchief thrown across her face and neck, I might have supposed her asleep. I rushed towards her, and embraced her with ardour; but the deadly languor and coldness of the limbs told me that what I now held in my arms had ceased to be the Elizabeth whom I had loved and cherished. The murderous mark of the fiend's grasp was on her neck, and the breath had ceased to issue from her lips.

While I still hung over her in the agony of despair, I happened to look up. The windows of the room had before been darkened, and I felt a kind of panic on seeing the pale yellow light of the moon illuminate the chamber. The shutters had been thrown back; and,

II : J. *Monster with victim. from* **Mysteries of Paris** *by Eugène Sue. This was a book of sensational horror stories which was very popular in the mid-nineteenth century.*

with a sensation of horror not to be described, I saw at the open window a figure the most hideous and abhorred. A grin was on the face of the monster; he seemed to jeer as with his fiendish finger he pointed towards the corpse of my wife. I rushed towards the window and, drawing a pistol from my bosom, fired; but he eluded me, leaped from his station, and, running with the swiftness of lightning, plunged into the lake.

18　　Now here, from *The Bride of Frankenstein*, is a particularly graphic account of the monster's treatment of a vulnerable victim. Notice in this extract how much is made of the strong sexual element in the fears aroused by the idea of such a powerful yet unnatural creature. The sexuality of the relationship between the monster and his victim, which was so underplayed in (*g*) is here openly exploited.

(*h*)　　And meanwhile, above the town, in the fields which bordered the dense pine forest, a young shepherdess was tending her sheep. They were drinking at a pond which lay under a small bluff, and on this bluff, overlooking her flock, the little shepherdess sat, swinging her legs.
　　She was looking across the hillside at the twinkling lights of the

town; at the winking yellow diamonds that were the windows of distant Castle Frankenstein.

So immersed was she in admiring the view (being, indeed, more than a little sleepy) that she did not see the tall gaunt form which came stumbling through the woods, and moving with the rolling gait of a drunken man.

A hundred yards away from where the girl sat dreaming, the figure stopped at a small waterfall; kneeling down by the side of the mountain rivulet, and scooping up the water in the palm of its hand; drinking ravenously, and grunting like an animal.

It stopped drinking, satiated, and the calm surface of the water showed him a face. It was white, and heavy, and scarred – and as he gazed he struck at it, shattering the image into a thousand fragments.

Then the Monster (for it was he) stumbled to his feet, and set off on his swaying run.

Branches brushed him, and clinging weeds impeded his progress, while brambles tore at face and hands. But always he went forward, with a blind purposefulness that brooked of no petty diversion.

At last the woods gave way to the open country, and as he crashed out of the pines he stood blinking uncertainly at the prospect before him.

To the left, high up on the hill, was the Castle: below, the twinkling lights of the town. On his right the meadows stretched for less than a mile, before the woodland began again. He turned to the right, and made his way across the fields, towards the bluff and the little pond.

As though sensing something unnatural in the stumbling shape that came so blindly among them, the sheep scattered with little cries of alarm, the old bell-wether trotting away far in advance of his flock.

On went the Monster towards the little bluff. His mouth was working, although no sounds came from it but a low gurgling: and his hands were waving like a penguin's flippers.

The shepherdess was patting a sheep that had thrust its muzzle against her soft thigh.

She sighed: it was so peaceful. The town going to sleep below, the nightingale beginning his song in woods behind her . . . Oh! She stretched her arms above her head, and glanced around.

Then she screamed . . . and screamed . . . and screamed again. She was looking only at the Monster as she rent the air with her shrieks, so that she stepped back from the bluff: the grass gave way beneath her feet on the very edge of the small cliff.

There was a shriek louder even than the others, and she plunged into the pool below.

The dark shape above watched her fall: watched her wild efforts as she struck out in the icy water.

It stood there chuckling for a long second. Then it leaped out, and in a moment it had joined the girl below.

She was fighting now: fighting drowning, and . . . something worse than drowning.

And now those steel arms had her tightly grasped: she struck at the white, glistening face with her tiny clenched fists. Struck, wildly, blindly; bruising it – gashing it with her nails.

And still that grasp did not relax, as she was borne towards the edge of the pool. . . .

It was an unconscious girl that the Monster threw down on the grass at the water's edge.

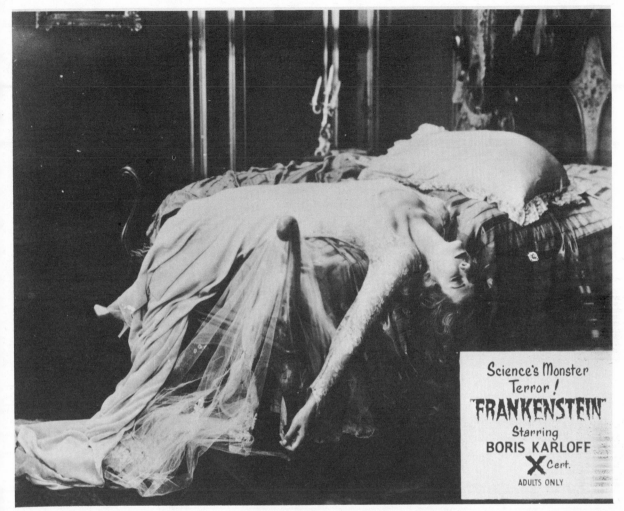

Science's Monster
Terror!
FRANKENSTEIN
Starring
BORIS KARLOFF
X Cert.
ADULTS ONLY

II:L. *The seductive victim. A publicity still for the 1931 film. Compare this with figure II:E.*

He surveyed the supine form at his feet, and grunted. He stirred it with his boot and it did not move. Still grunting, he dropped on his knees beside the girl's body, and took one cold hand in his. He stroked her face, an unknown emotion sending a pleasant warmth through his body.

The girl opened her eyes, uncomprehending. She blinked her eyes: and then, as she saw the face bending over her, she screamed again.

The Monster pawed her face, and the girl shrank back.

"Don't touch me!"

There was a growl, as the clumsy hand sought her face once more.

A scream; and this time, as though human reason were breaking beneath a burden of horror unbearable.

Two hunters who were passing through the woods stopped as they heard the scream.

"What was that, August?"

"I don't know, Heinrich. What did *you* think it was?"

"To me," said August, the younger of the two, "it sounded like a woman's cry."

Heinrich shook his head.

II:K. *The monster is isolated from everybody. Boris Karloff.*

"A cat, I think. They sound very human."

"That's true," said the other, resuming his walk.

Then, clearly through the night air, came another shriek; and this time they could hear a girl's voice sobbing with horror.

"A woman, August, in trouble. Quick."

They turned and ran through the woods.

"Is your gun loaded, Heinrich? Mine isn't."

"Yes.... Oh, look! It's a woman ... August, load quickly. As God's my judge, it's the Monster!"

The other man brought his gun to his shoulder, shouting to draw the Monster away from the girl. Both men could see that the creature had clapped his hand across the girl's mouth: but her flailing arms and kicking legs told them that at least she was not dead.

What other injuries she might have sustained they did not dare consider.

III Dr Jekyll and Mr Hyde

1   Probably the most powerful theme in *Frankenstein* was the relationship between Frankenstein and the monster. It was Frankenstein who created the monster, yet for most of the story they were bitterly opposed to each other. It is impossible really to think of either of them without the other. It is the existence of each other which gives meaning and purpose to their lives. It is almost as if Frankenstein and the monster were two parts of a single personality. Perhaps that is another reason for the confusion about who the name Frankenstein refers to (II : 1). They are necessary for each other's existences and in the end they are equal victims.

2   This idea is taken a stage further in *The Strange Case of Dr Jekyll and Mr Hyde*. Instead of two separate people who depend on each other so much that they come to *seem* like one, here there are two apparently separate people who *really* are separate aspects of one single person. Just as Frankenstein and the monster are superficially very different from each other, so Dr Jekyll and Mr Hyde appear at first sight to be poles apart. The conflict comes not from linking together two similar personalities, but in binding together two personalities which are *mutually exclusive*. Neither one can tolerate the existence of the other, yet each needs the other to survive. Thus, they are locked in a continual struggle, which can only end in the eventual destruction of them both.

3   The trouble with a story as familiar as *Jekyll and Hyde* is that it is almost impossible now to imagine what its effect might be upon somebody who had never heard of it. The two names are linked together even for people who have no idea what they originally refer to. What this means is that when we actually read the book or see one of the films based upon it, we already know the secret of the story. Jekyll and Hyde are the same person, however different they may seem. The films indeed often rely upon the assumption that the audience understands this secret. Yet in Stevenson's original story, we do not learn it until nearly three-quarters of the way through the book. There is never any shock now. What there is must be fascination. Fascination with what is known but not understood and therefore is still frightening.

4   *The Strange Case of Dr Jekyll and Mr Hyde* was written seventy years after *Frankenstein*. Robert Louis Stevenson, who also wrote *Kidnapped* and *Treasure Island*, was born in Edinburgh in 1850. He shared with most other Scottish writers a deep interest, amounting almost to an obsession, in conscience and the problem of evil. Because of the strictness of his upbringing, Stevenson seems to have felt a desire to experience and

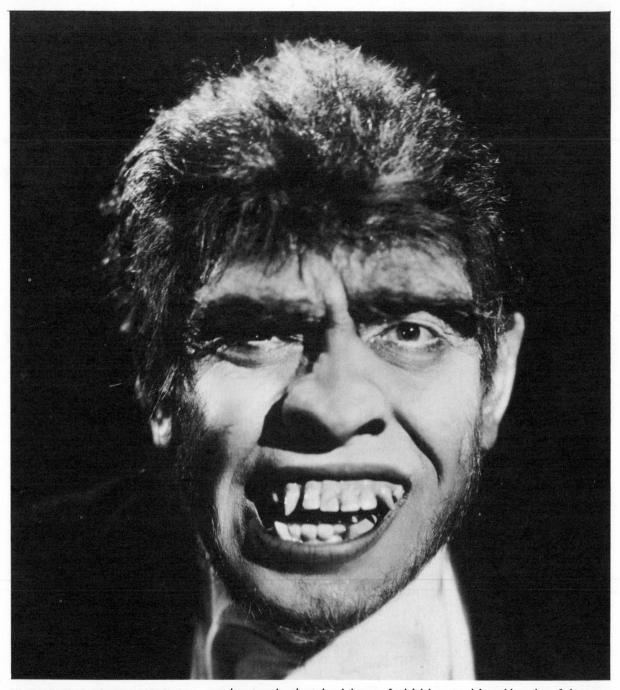

III : A. *Frederic March as Mr Hyde in the 1932 film of the book.*

understand what had been forbidden to him. He also felt very strongly about the hypocrisy of so-called respectable people who really led disreputable private lives. After he had finished *Jekyll and Hyde*, Stevenson said: "I had long been trying to write a story on this subject, to find a body or vehicle, for that strong sense of *man's double being* which must at times come in upon and overwhelm the mind of every thinking creature."

5   The idea for the story eventually came to Stevenson in a dream. He complained to his wife that she had wakened him from dreaming "a fine bogey tale". At daybreak he began writing and had completed the first draft in a few days. The book was written, rewritten twice and printed, all within ten weeks.

6   Stevenson's interest in the idea of a double life began when he heard the story of Deacon Brodie, who was by day a highly respectable city councillor and Deacon of the Incorporation of Edinburgh Wrights and Masons, and was by night the leader of a notorious gang of burglars. As a young man, Stevenson wrote a melodrama about Deacon Brodie and there can be no doubt that he was a kind of prototype figure for *Jekyll and Hyde*. Although the setting of *Jekyll and Hyde* is supposed to be London, the

III : B. *Deacon Brodie (on right) meeting his accomplice George Smith for the first time. From John Kay's A Series of Original Portraits, which also contains a brief biography of Deacon Brodie.*

atmosphere is identical to early nineteenth-century Edinburgh with its respectability and its underworld, both of which Stevenson knew. Thus, the setting and the morality of the story are both particularly Scottish. The amazing thing about *Jekyll and Hyde* is how it goes far beyond its Scottish origins and becomes a kind of parable about the general condition of man.

7   *The Strange Case of Dr Jekyll and Mr Hyde* is in the form of a *novella*, which is something between a short novel and a long story. It is quite complicated, because it contains sections of narrative spoken by different characters and from different points of view. Mr Utterson (a lawyer) and Dr Lanyon are both worried about a mutual friend of theirs called Dr Henry Jekyll. Dr Jekyll seems to have become friendly with a man called Edward Hyde, whom nobody really knows anything about and who seems to be a thoroughly disreputable character. Everyone who meets him takes an instant violent dislike to him. Dr Jekyll and Mr Hyde have never actually been seen together, but they both use Dr Jekyll's house and in his will Dr Jekyll has left all his money to Mr Hyde. Mr Hyde's reputation for evil deeds grows until one day he is seen sadistically murdering an old man. The police are, however, unable to trace the culprit. For a brief time afterwards, Dr Jekyll becomes particularly active in public and charitable works and then suddenly lapses into a life of total seclusion, refusing to see anyone at all. During this period, Mr Utterson goes one evening to see Dr Lanyon, who is in a state of acute despair which appears to have been caused by Dr Jekyll. He will not say exactly what has happened, but when a few weeks later he dies, Mr Utterson receives a letter which is not to be opened until the disappearance of Dr Jekyll.

8   Some time later, Dr Jekyll's butler, Poole, arrives unexpectedly at Mr Utterson's house, begging him to accompany him back to Dr Jekyll's, because he fears his master has been murdered. He has not been seen for a long time, even by his own servants and has communicated with them only in writing. One day, Poole, coming into the lecture theatre which leads into Dr Jekyll's study, saw somebody rummaging about among the crates of chemicals there. It was not Jekyll, but Mr Hyde, who ran off into the study as soon as he saw Poole. Mr Utterson agrees to sort matters out and tries to talk to Dr Jekyll through the door of the study. The voice which replies, begging him to leave, is also Hyde's. They break down the door. As they do so, Hyde commits suicide. They can find no trace of Dr Jekyll. Instead, they find a sealed letter from him, addressed to Mr Utterson.

9   Mr Utterson first reads the letter from Dr Lanyon. In it, Dr Lanyon describes how Dr Jekyll once wrote to him asking him to fetch some chemicals from Jekyll's house for him. These were later collected by Mr Hyde who, with Dr Lanyon watching, mixed them together, swallowed the mixture and, after a brief paroxysm, was transformed into Dr Jekyll. Mr Utterson then reads

the letter from Dr Jekyll himself. It contains the story of his life, describing his beliefs in the double nature of self which lead him to experiment until he discovered a certain mixture which would transform him and allow the evil, cruel side of his character (which he had always kept in check) to become free. It transformed him physically into a new person, whom he called Edward Hyde. So Dr Jekyll lived a double life: he was both Henry Jekyll the respectable doctor and Edward Hyde the sadistic murderer. Gradually, however, Jekyll found that Hyde was beginning to take over more and more. Sometimes he fell asleep as Jekyll and awoke as Hyde. In the end he had used up all the chemicals in keeping Hyde at bay and he was unable to buy fresh supplies. In his last period as Dr Jekyll, he wrote the letter to Mr Utterson.

10　　As can be seen from that summary of the story, the part that people remember is really only the ending. The letters which Mr Utterson reads, which contain the explanation of the mystery, are by far the strongest and most compelling part of the book. The beginning, although it contains some passages of fine writing and some effective descriptions, is just "a fine bogey tale". What it does is rather like the beginning of a Hitchcock thriller, where the suspense is gradually built up and up until it just has to explode. The reason that I have given such a full summary of the book is so that you can see how Stevenson manages to keep his readers guessing or, if they know the secret, how he manages to delay the moment when he confirms that they are right. This description which follows could be instructions for the art director of a film, so keen and atmospheric is the visual sense, so tailored to maintain suspense.

(a)　　　　It was by this time about nine in the morning, and the first fog of the season. A great chocolate-coloured pall lowered over heaven, but the wind was continually charging and routing these embattled vapours; so that as the cab crawled from street to street, Mr Utterson beheld a marvellous number of degrees and hues of twilight; for here it would be dark like the back-end of evening; and there would be a glow of a rich, lurid brown, like the light of some strange conflagration; and here, for a moment, the fog would be quite broken up, and a haggard shaft of daylight would glance in between the swirling wreaths. The dismal quarter of Soho seen under these changing glimpses, with its muddy ways, and slatternly passengers, and its lamps, which had never been extinguished or had been kindled afresh to combat this mournful reinvasion of darkness, seemed, in the lawyer's eyes, like a district of some city in a nightmare. The thoughts of his mind, besides, were of the gloomiest dye; and when he glanced at the companion of his drive, he was conscious of some touch of that terror of the law and the law's officers, which may at times assail the most honest.

As the cab drew up before the address indicated, the fog lifted a little and showed him a dingy street, a gin palace, a low French eating-house, a shop for the retail of penny numbers and two-penny salads, many ragged children huddled in the doorways, and many women of many different nationalities passing out, key in hand, to have a morning glass; and the next moment the fog settled down again upon that part, as brown as umber, and cut him off from his blackguardly surroundings. This was the home of Henry Jekyll's favourite; of a man who was heir to quarter of a million sterling.

11   We first hear anything about Mr Hyde in a description by Mr Utterson's cousin Mr Enfield of an incident he had seen. Only later do we learn Hyde's identity for certain.

(*b*)   "Well, it was this way," returned Mr Enfield: "I was coming home from some place at the end of the world, about three o'clock of a black winter morning, and my way lay through a part of town where there was literally nothing to be seen but lamps. Street after street, and all the folks asleep — street after street, all lighted up as if for a procession and all as empty as a church — till at last I got into that state of mind when a man listens and listens and begins to long for

III:C.   Nineteenth-century Edinburgh. This is a photograph by Thomas Keith of the corner of the West Bow and the Lawnmarket.

III : D. *The backstreet world of Hyde. This photograph (of Bakehouse Close, Canongate, Edinburgh) is also by Thomas Keith.*

the sight of a policeman. All at once, I saw two figures: one a little man who was stumping along eastward at a good walk, and the other a girl of maybe eight or ten who was running as hard as she was able down a cross street. Well, sir, the two ran into one another naturally enough at the corner; and then came the horrible part of the thing; for the man trampled calmly over the child's body and left her screaming on the ground. It sounds nothing to hear, but it was hellish to see. It wasn't like a man; it was like some damned Juggernaut. I gave a view halloa, took to my heels, collared my gentleman, and brought him back to where there was already quite a group about the screaming child. He was perfectly cool and made no resistance, but gave me one look, so ugly that it brought out the sweat on me like running.

The people who had turned out were the girl's own family; and pretty soon, the doctor, for whom she had been sent, put in his appearance. Well, the child was not much the worse, more frightened, according to the Sawbones; and there you might have supposed would be an end to it. But there was one curious circumstance. I had taken a loathing to my gentleman at first sight. So had the child's family, which was only natural. But the doctor's case was what struck me. He was the usual cut-and-dry apothecary, of no particular age and colour, with a strong Edinburgh accent, and about as emotional as a bagpipe. Well, sir, he was like the rest of us; every time he looked at my prisoner, I saw that Sawbones turn sick and white with the desire to kill him. I knew what was in his mind, just as he knew what was in mine; and killing being out of the question, we did the next best. We told the man we could and would make such a scandal out of this, as should make his name stink from one end of London to the other. If he had any friends or any credit, we undertook that he should lose them. And all the time, as we were pitching it in red hot, we were keeping the women off him as best we could, for they were as wild as harpies.

I never saw a circle of such hateful faces; and there was the man in the middle, with a kind of black, sneering coolness – frightened too, I could see that – but carrying it off, sir, really like Satan. 'If you choose to make capital out of this accident,' said he, 'I am naturally helpless. No gentleman but wishes to avoid a scene,' says he. 'Name your figure.' Well, we screwed him up to a hundred pounds for the child's family; he would have clearly liked to stick out; but there was something about the lot of us that meant mischief, and at last he struck.

The next thing was to get the money; and where do you think he carried us but to that place with the door? – whipped out a key, went in, and presently came back with the matter of ten pounds in gold and a cheque for the balance on Coutts's, drawn payable to bearer and signed with a name that I can't mention, though it's one of the points of my story, but it was a name at least very well known and often printed. The figure was stiff; but the signature was good for more than that, if it was only genuine. I took the liberty of pointing out to my gentleman that the whole business looked apocryphal, and that a man does not, in real life, walk into a cellar door at four in the morning and come out of it with another man's cheque for close upon a hundred pounds. But he was quite easy and sneering. 'Set your mind at rest,' says he, 'I will stay with you till the banks open and cash the cheque myself.' So we all set off, the doctor, and the child's father, and our friend and myself, and passed the rest of the night in my chambers; and next day, when we had breakfasted, went in a body to the bank. I gave in the cheque myself, and said I had every reason to believe it was a forgery. Not a bit of it. The cheque was genuine."

12   Although that incident does not give you a very savoury impression of Mr Hyde, there is nothing about it to suggest that he is anything other than a brutal maniac. The same is true of the

III : E. *Robert Louis Stevenson.*

description of the murder of the old man. It is not until Dr Lanyon's letter that Hyde's identity and Jekyll's secret are simultaneously revealed. Here is the section in which Dr Lanyon, having obtained the chemicals for Dr Jekyll, awaits the arrival of his "messenger".

(c)　　　Twelve o'clock had scarce rung out over London, ere the knocker sounded very gently on the door. I went myself at the summons, and found a small man crouching against the pillars of the portico.

"Are you come from Dr Jekyll?" I asked.

He told me "yes" by a constrained gesture; and when I had bidden him enter, he did not obey me without a searching backward glance into the darkness of the square. There was a policeman not far off, advancing with his bull's-eye open; and at the sight, I thought my visitor started and made greater haste.

31

These particulars struck me, I confess, disagreeably; and as I followed him into the bright light of the consulting-room, I kept my hand ready on my weapon. Here, at last, I had a chance of clearly seeing him. I had never set eyes on him before, so much was certain. He was small, as I have said; I was struck besides with the shocking expression of his face, with his remarkable combination of great muscular activity and great apparent debility of constitution, and — last but not least — with the odd, subjective disturbance caused by his neighbourhood. This bore some resemblance to incipient rigour, and was accompanied by a marked sinking of the pulse. At the time, I set it down to some idiosyncratic, personal distaste, and merely wondered at the acuteness of the symptoms; but I have since had reason to believe the cause to lie much deeper in the nature of man, and to turn on some nobler hinge than the principle of hatred.

This person (who had thus, from the first moment of his entrance, struck in me what I can only describe as a disgustful curiosity) was dressed in a fashion that would have made an ordinary person laughable; his clothes, that is to say, although they were of rich and sober fabric, were enormously too large for him in eve•y measurement — the trousers hanging on his legs and rolled up to keep them from the ground, the waist of the coat below his haunches, and the collar sprawling wide upon his shoulders. Strange to relate, this ludicrous accoutrement was far from moving me to laughter. Rather, as there was something abnormal and misbegotten in the very essence of the creature that now faced me — something seizing, surprising, and revolting — this fresh disparity seemed but to fit in with and to reinforce it; so that to my interest in the man's nature and character, there was added a curiosity as to his origin, his life, his fortune and status in the world.

These observations, though they have taken so great a space to be set down in, were yet the work of a few seconds. My visitor was, indeed, on fire with sombre excitement.

"Have you got it?" he cried. "Have you got it?" And so lively was his impatience that he even laid his hand upon my arm and sought to shake me.

I put him back, conscious at his touch of a certain icy pang along my blood. "Come, sir," said I. "You forget that I have not yet the pleasure of your acquaintance. Be seated, if you please." and I showed him an example, and sat down myself in my customary seat and with as fair an imitation of my ordinary manner to a patient, as the lateness of the hour, the nature of my preoccupations, and the horror I had of my visitor, would suffer me to muster.

"I beg your pardon, Dr Lanyon," he replied civilly enough. "What you say is very well founded; and my impatience has shown its heels to any politeness. I come here at the instance of your colleague, Dr Henry Jekyll, on a piece of business of some moment; and I understood . . ." He paused and put his hand to his throat, and I could see, in spite of his collected manner, that he was wrestling against the approaches of the hysteria — "I understood, a drawer . . ."

But here I took pity on my visitor's suspense, and some perhaps on my own growing curiosity.

"There it is, sir," said I, pointing to the drawer, where it lay on the floor behind a table and still covered with the sheet.

He sprang to it, and then paused, and laid his hand upon his heart: I could hear his teeth grate with the convulsive action of his jaws; and his face was so ghastly to see that I grew alarmed both for his life and reason.

"Compose yourself," said I.

He turned a dreadful smile to me, and as if with the decision of despair, plucked away the sheet. At sight of the contents, he uttered one loud sob of such immense relief that I sat petrified. And the next moment, in a voice that was already fairly well under control, "Have you a graduated glass?" he asked.

I rose from my place with something of an effort and gave him what he asked.

He thanked me with a smiling nod, measured out a few minims of the red tincture and added one of the powders. The mixture, which was at first of a reddish hue, began, in proportion as the crystals melted, to brighten in colour, to effervesce audibly, and to throw off small fumes of vapour. Suddenly and at the same moment, the ebullition ceased and the compound changed to a dark purple, which faded again more slowly to a watery green. My visitor, who had watched these metamorphoses with a keen eye, smiled, set down the glass upon the table, and then turned and looked upon me with an air of scrutiny.

"And now," said he, "to settle what remains. Will you be wise? will you be guided? will you suffer me to take this glass in my hand and to go forth from your house without further parley? or has the greed of curiosity too much command of you? Think before you answer, for it shall be done as you decide. As you decide, you shall be left as you were before, and neither richer nor wiser, unless the sense of service rendered to a man in mortal distress may be counted as a kind of riches of the soul. Or, if you shall so prefer to choose, a new province of knowledge and new avenues to fame and power shall be laid open to you, here, in this room, upon the instant; and your sight shall be blasted by a prodigy to stagger the unbelief of Satan."

"Sir," said I, affecting a coolness that I was far from truly possessing, "you speak enigmas, and you will perhaps not wonder that I hear you with no very strong impression of belief. But I have gone too far in the way of inexplicable services to pause before I see the end."

"It is well," replied my visitor. "Lanyon, you remember your vows: what follows is under the seal of our profession. And now, you who have so long been bound to the most narrow and material views, you who have denied the virtue of transcendental medicine, you who have derided your superiors — behold!"

He put the glass to his lips and drank at one gulp. A cry followed; he reeled, staggered, clutched at the table and held on, staring with injected eyes, gasping with open mouth; and as I looked there came, I thought, a change — he seemed to swell — his face became suddenly black and the features seemed to melt and alter — and the next moment I had sprung to my feet and leaped back against the wall, my arm raised to shield me from that prodigy, my mind submerged in terror.

"O God!" I screamed, and "O God!" again and again; for there before my eyes — pale and shaken, and half fainting, and groping before him with his hands, like a man restored from death — there stood Henry Jekyll!

13   This passage shows a return to a theme which we have already looked at in the case of *Frankenstein* — the mad scientist. The same feeling of panic at the awful possibilities of experimental science is coupled with the same fascination in its apparently limitless power. The moral of the story, that care should be

III : F. *The mad scientist in his lab-oratory prepares the drug.*

taken not to lose control, is perhaps modified by Stevenson's excitement at what happens when control is lost. Here is Dr Jekyll's description of the sequence of experiments by which he came to achieve his double identity.

(d)   I was so far in my reflections when, as I have said, a side light began to shine upon the subject from the laboratory table. I began to perceive more deeply than it has ever yet been stated, the trembling immateriality, the mist-like transcience, of this seemingly so solid body in which we walk attired. Certain agents I found to have the power to shake and to pluck back that fleshly vestment, even as a wind might toss the curtains of a pavilion. For two good reasons, I will not enter deeply into this scientific branch of my confession. First, because I have been made to learn that the doom and burthen of our life is bound for ever on man's shoulders, and when the attempt is made to cast it off, it but returns upon us with more unfamiliar and more awful pressure. Second, because, as my narrative will make, alas! too evident, my discoveries were incomplete. Enough, then, that I not only recognised my natural body for the mere aura and effulgence of certain of the powers that made up my spirit, but managed to compound a drug by which these powers should be dethroned from their supremacy, and a second form and countenance substituted, none the less natural to me because they were the expression, and bore the stamp, of lower elements in my soul.

I hesitated long before I put this theory to the test of practice. I knew well that I risked death; for any drug that so potently controlled and shook the very fortress of identity, might by the least scruple of an overdose or at the least inopportunity in the moment of exhibition, utterly blot out that immaterial tabernacle which I looked to it to change. But the temptation of a discovery so singular and profound, at last overcame the suggestions of alarm. I had long since prepared my tincture; I purchased at once, from a firm of wholesale chemists, a large quantity of a particular salt which I

III : G. *Harry Benham in the 1912 version of* Jekyll and Hyde.

knew, from my experiments, to be the last ingredient required; and late one accursed night, I compounded the elements, watched them boil and smoke together in the glass, and when the ebullition had subsided, with a strong glow of courage, drank off the potion.

The most racking pangs succeeded: a grinding in the bones, deadly nausea, and a horror of the spirit that cannot be exceeded at the hour of birth or death. Then these agonies began swiftly to subside, and I came to myself as if out of a great sickness. There was something strange in my sensations, something indescribably new and, from its very novelty, incredibly sweet. I felt younger, lighter, happier in body; within I was conscious of a heady reck-lessness, a current of disordered sensual images running like a mill race in my fancy, a solution of the bonds of obligation, an unknown but not an innocent freedom of the soul. I knew myself, at the first breath of this new life, to be more wicked, tenfold more wicked, sold a slave to my original evil; and the thought, in that moment, braced and delighted me like wine. I stretched out my hands, exulting in the freshness of these sensations; and in the act, I was suddenly aware that I had lost in stature.

There was no mirror, at that date, in my room; that which stands beside me as I write, was brought there later on for the very purpose of these transformations. The night, however, was far gone into the morning — the morning, black as it was, was nearly ripe for the conception of the day — the inmates of my house were locked in the most rigorous hours of slumber; and I determined, flushed as I was with hope and triumph, to venture in my new shape as far as to my bedroom. I crossed the yard, wherein the constellations looked down upon me, I could have thought, with wonder, the first creature of that sort that their unsleeping vigilance had yet disclosed to them; I stole through the corridors, a stranger in my own house; and coming to my room, I saw for the first time the appearance of Edward Hyde.

I must here speak by theory alone, saying not that which I know, but that which I suppose to be most probable. The evil side of my nature, to which I had now transferred the stamping efficacy, was less robust and less developed than the good which I had just deposed. Again, in the course of my life, which had been, after all, nine-tenths a life of effort, virtue, and control, it had been much less exercised and much less exhausted. And hence, as I think, it came about that Edward Hyde was so much smaller, slighter, and younger than Henry Jekyll. Even as good shone upon the countenance of the one, evil was written broadly and plainly on the face of the other. Evil besides (which I must still believe to be the lethal side of man) had left on that body an imprint of deformity and decay. And yet when I looked upon that ugly idol in the glass, I was conscious of no repugnance, rather of a leap of welcome. This, too, was myself. It seemed natural and human. In my eyes it bore a livelier image of the spirit, it seemed more express and single, than the imperfect and divided countenance I had been hitherto accustomed to call mine. And in so far I was doubtless right. I have observed that when I wore the semblance of Edward Hyde, none could come near to me at first without a visible misgiving of the flesh. This, as I take it, was because all human beings, as we meet them, are commingled out of good and evil: and Edward Hyde, alone in the ranks of mankind, was pure evil.

I lingered but a moment at the mirror: the second and conclusive experiment had yet to be attempted; it yet remained to be seen if I had lost my identity beyond redemption and must flee before day-light from a house that was no longer mine; and hurrying back to my

III : H. *John Barrymore in the 1920 film.*

cabinet, I once more prepared and drank the cup, once more suffered the pangs of dissolution, and came to myself once more with the character, the stature, and the face of Henry Jekyll.

14   Just as with *Frankenstein*, the mad scientist aspect of *Jekyll and Hyde* was one which the films based on the book chose to concentrate upon. The first film version of the story was released as early as 1908 by the Selig Polyscope Company of Chicago. Another four versions were made during the next ten years, including one in which the last scene, in order to provide a happy ending, revealed that the whole thing was only a ghastly dream of Dr Jekyll's.

15   It was in 1920 that the cinematic potential of the story was first really exploited. Obviously, transformations are ideally suited to being filmed in close-up and it is amazing how much the actor John Barrymore, who played the lead role in 1920, was able to achieve just by dislocating his facial muscles, before the camera

III : J. *Hyde with his victim.*
Frederic March and Miriam
Hopkins in Mamoulian's film.

cut away to let the make-up department get to work on him. The
film's most significant departure from Stevenson's story was
one which most later films were also to follow — namely, to give
Dr Jekyll a superior girlfriend/wife and Mr Hyde at least one
pathetic mistress/victim. By far the most impressive film of *Dr
Jekyll and Mr Hyde* was made in 1932 by Rouben Mamoulian. He
used an undisclosed technique to enable the transformation from
Jekyll into Hyde to take place apparently continuously in front of
the camera. The process is accompanied by an overpowering
soundtrack, which includes amplified heartbeats, reversed gongs
and light frequencies photographed onto the soundtrack. The
total effect is probably as close as cinema can come to recreat-
ing for us what it *feels* like (not just what it *looks* like) to change
from Jekyll into Hyde, to experience what Stevenson called "the
war in the members"

16   No subsequent version of *Jekyll and Hyde* has been able to
match Mamoulian's, either for the comprehensiveness of its
effects or the careful balance of plot. The character of Ivy, the girl
Hyde sets up as his mistress, is used not just for box office
appeal, but in order to develop the composite character of Jekyll
and Hyde. In this film, there can be no doubt that, however cruel
Hyde may be, he does also represent a positive *life force* which is

set against Jekyll's prudery. In 1941, Metro-Goldwyn-Mayer released what was really just a re-make of Mamoulian's film, with Spencer Tracy and Ingrid Bergman. The film is, however, heavy and much too wordy. The inevitable Hammer version, *The Two Faces of Dr Jekyll*, made in 1960 with Paul Massie, plays up the sexual aspects of the story, which are all suppressed in Stevenson, and in many ways serves to make it less frightening. There have been other, less notable attempts to make films on this general theme, including a *Son of Dr Jekyll* and a *Daughter of Dr Jekyll*, but the only one which deserves mention is Jerry Lewis's parody of the story, and the whole mad scientist idea, in *The Nutty Professor*, a hilarious film made in 1963. There have also been more psychological treatments of the theme, the most famous being Hitchcock's *Psycho*, which some people believe is the most frightening film ever made.

17   Of course, one of the reasons why *Jekyll and Hyde* converts so easily into cinema is that the distinction between good and evil is, at least at first sight, so clear. Dr Jekyll is good; Mr Hyde is

III:K. *Spencer Tracy as Dr Jekyll in his laboratory.*

evil. We have already seen, however, in Mamoulian's film, how Mr Hyde is both evil and at the same time a life force or source of positive energy. He may feel only sadistic impulses, but at least he does feel. As for Dr Jekyll, his persistent goodness can easily lapse into self-righteousness; his virtue can easily be seen as nothing more than respectability. Even in Elizabethan times, people believed that man was a fatal mixture of half angel and half animal, and could tend in either direction. A close look at Stevenson's story soon reveals that the distinction is not necessarily the black and white contrast that is often assumed. In any case, is it not true to say that any portrait of consistent virtue is almost by definition boring? Is it not true that we prefer to read about people who are in some way guilty of doing wrong? Most of us, like Stevenson was, are fascinated by what is forbidden. The reason that *Dr Jekyll and Mr Hyde* can be called a modern myth is quite simply that we all share the conflict which confronts Jekyll. The story does not present a solution. All it does is to show us where that conflict can lead. Here is the beginning of Dr Jekyll's letter to Mr Utterson.

(e) I was born in the year 18— to a large fortune, endowed besides with excellent parts, inclined by nature to industry, fond of the respect of the wise and good among my fellow-men, and thus, as might have been supposed, with every guarantee of an honourable and distinguished future. And indeed the worst of my faults was a certain impatient gaiety of disposition, such as has made the happiness of many, but such as I found it hard to reconcile with my imperious desire to carry my head high, and wear a more than commonly grave countenance before the public.

Hence it came about that I concealed my pleasures; and that when I reached years of reflection, and began to look round me and take stock of my progress and position in the world, I stood already committed to a profound duplicity of life. Many a man would have even blazoned such irregularities as I was guilty of; but from the high views that I had set before me, I regarded and hid them with an almost morbid sense of shame. It was thus rather the exacting nature of my aspirations than any particular degradation in my faults, that made me what I was, and, with even a deeper trench than in the majority of men, severed in me those provinces of good and ill which divide and compound man's dual nature. In this case, I was driven to reflect deeply and inveterately on that hard law of life, which lies at the root of religion and is one of the most plentiful springs of distress.

Though so profound a double-dealer, I was in no sense a hypocrite; both sides of me were in dead earnest; I was no more myself when I laid aside restraint and plunged in shame, than when I laboured, in the eye of day, at the furtherance of knowledge or the relief of sorrow and suffering. And it chanced that the direction of my scientific studies, which led wholly towards the mystic and the transcendental, reacted and shed a strong light on this consciousness of the perennial war among my members.

With every day, and from both sides of my intelligence, the moral and the intellectual, I thus drew steadily nearer to that truth, by whose partial discovery I have been doomed to such a dreadful shipwreck: that man is not truly one, but truly two. I say two, because the state of my own knowledge does not pass beyond that point. Others will follow, others will outstrip me on the same lines; and I hazard the guess that man will be ultimately known for a mere polity of multifarious, incongruous and independent denizens. I for my part, from the nature of my life, advanced infallibly in one direction and in one direction only.

It was on the moral side, and in my own person, that I learned to recognize the thorough and primitive duality of man; I saw that, of the two natures that contended in the field of my consciousness, even if I could rightly be said to be either, it was only because I was radically both; and from an early date, even before the course of my scientific discoveries had begun to suggest the most naked possibility of such a miracle, I had learned to dwell with pleasure, as a beloved day-dream, on the thought of the separation of these elements.

If each, I told myself, could but be housed in separate identities, life would be relieved of all that was unbearable; the unjust might go his way, delivered from the aspirations and remorse of his more upright twin; and the just could walk steadfastly and securely on his upward path, doing the good things in which he found his pleasure, and no longer exposed to disgrace and penitence by the hands of this extraneous evil. It was the curse of mankind that these incongruous faggots were thus bound together – that in the agonised womb of consciousness, these polar twins should be continuously struggling. How, then, were they dissociated?

18   That description is similar to a feeling which most people experience in a mild sort of way. When this feeling of having more than one personality becomes extreme, it is called *schizophrenia*, or split personality. *Jekyll and Hyde* is about the effects of schizophrenia. It is also about the desire of a single personality to project itself in more than one way.

(*e*)   This familiar that I called out of my own soul, and sent forth alone to do his good pleasure, was a being inherently malign and villainous; his every act and thought centred on self; drinking pleasure with bestial avidity from any degree of torture to another; relentless like a man of stone. Henry Jekyll stood at times aghast before the acts of Edward Hyde; but the situation was apart from ordinary laws, and insidiously relaxed the grasp of conscience. It was Hyde, after all, and Hyde alone, that was guilty. Jekyll was no worse; he woke again to his good qualities seemingly unimpaired; he would even make haste, where it was possible, to undo the evil done by Hyde. And thus his conscience slumbered.

19   At first, Jekyll is the carrier and Hyde is the virus. But soon the personality which had been suppressed begins to take over. Hyde grows in strength and begins to dominate Jekyll. The question which emerges is whether the respectable Dr Jekyll is any more the *real* personality than the bestial Mr Hyde. Who is the real Henry Jekyll?

(*f*)   Some two months before the murder of Sir Danvers, I had been out for one of my adventures, had returned at a late hour, and woke the next day in bed with somewhat odd sensations. It was in vain I

III : L. In this frame from an American horror comic, the hero is suffering from an overdose of LSD which has had the same sort of effect on him as Dr Jekyll's mixture.

looked about me; in vain I saw the decent furniture and tall proportions of my room in the square; in vain that I recognised the pattern of the bed curtains and the design of the mahogany frame; something still kept insisting that I was not where I was, that I had not wakened where I seemed to be, but in the little room in Soho where I was accustomed to sleep in the body of Edward Hyde. I smiled to myself, and, in my psychological way began lazily to inquire into the elements of this illusion, occasionally, even as I did so, dropping back into a comfortable morning doze.

I was still so engaged when, in one of my more wakeful moments, my eyes fell upon my hand. Now the hand of Henry Jekyll (as you have often remarked) was professional in shape and size: it was large, firm, white, and comely. But the hand which I now saw, clearly enough, in the yellow light of a mid-London morning, lying half shut on the bed clothes, was lean, corded, knuckly, of a dusky pallor, and thickly shaded with a swart growth of hair. It was the hand of Edward Hyde.

I must have stared upon it for near half a minute, sunk as I was in the mere stupidity of wonder, before terror woke up in my breast as sudden and startling as the crash of cymbals; and bounding from my bed, I rushed to the mirror. At the sight that met my eyes, my blood was changed into something exquisitely thin and icy. Yes, I had gone to bed Henry Jekyll, I had awakened Edward Hyde. How was this to be explained? I asked myself; and then, with another bound of terror – how was it to be remedied? It was well on in the morning; the servants were up; all my drugs were in the cabinet – a long journey down two pair of stairs, through the back passage, across the open court and through the anatomical theatre, from where I was then standing horror-struck. It might indeed be possible to cover my face; but of what use was that, when I was unable to conceal the alteration in my stature?

And then with an overpowering sweetness of relief, it came back upon my mind that the servants were already used to the coming and going of my second self. I had soon dressed, as well as I was able, in clothes of my own size; had soon passed through the house, where Bradshaw stared and drew back at seeing Mr Hyde at such an hour and in such a strange array; and ten minutes later, Dr Jekyll had returned to his own shape and was sitting down, with a darkened brow, to make a feint of breakfasting.

Small indeed was my appetite. This inexplicable incident, this reversal of my previous experience, seemed, like the Babylonian finger on the wall, to be spelling out the letters of my judgment; and I began to reflect more seriously than ever before on the issues and possibilities of my double existence. That part of me which I had the power of projecting, had lately been much exercised and nourished; it had seemed to me of late as though the body of Edward Hyde had grown in stature, as though (when I wore that form) I were conscious of a more generous tide of blood; and I began to spy a danger that, if this were much prolonged, the balance of my nature might be permanently overthrown, the power of voluntary change be forfeited, and the character of Edward Hyde become irrevocably mine.

The power of the drug had not been always equally displayed. Once, very early in my career, it had totally failed me; since then I had been obliged on more than one occasion to double, and once, with infinite risk of death, to treble the amount; and these rare uncertainties had cast hitherto the sole shadow on my contentment. Now, however, and in the light of that morning's accident, I was led to remark that whereas, in the beginning, the difficulty had been to throw off the body of Jekyll, it had of late gradually but decidedly transferred itself to the other side. All things therefore seemed to point to this: that I was slowly losing hold of my original and better self, and becoming slowly incorporated with my second and worse.

Between these two, I now felt I had to choose. My two natures had memory in common, but all other faculties were most unequally shared between them. Jekyll (who was composite) now with the most sensitive apprehensions, now with a greedy gusto, projected and shared in the pleasures and adventures of Hyde; but Hyde was indifferent to Jekyll, or but remembered him as the mountain bandit remembers the cavern in which he conceals himself from pursuit. Jekyll had more than a father's interest; Hyde had more than a son's indifference. To cast in my lot with Jekyll, was to die to those appetites which I had long secretly indulged and had of late begun to pamper. To cast it in with Hyde, was to die to a thousand interests and aspirations, and to become, at a blow and for ever, despised and friendless.

The bargain might appear unequal; but there was still another consideration in the scales; for while Jekyll would suffer smartingly in the fires of abstinence, Hyde would be not even conscious of all that he had lost. Strange as my circumstances were, the terms of this debate are as old and commonplace as man; much the same inducements and alarms cast the die for any tempted and trembling sinner; and it fell out with me, as it falls with so vast a majority of my fellows, that I chose the better part and was found wanting in the strength to keep to it.

20   The idea of everybody having a double, or *Doppelgänger*, was common throughout Europe in the nineteenth century. In 1824 another Scotsman called James Hogg had written *The Private Memoirs and Confessions of a Justified Sinner*, in which the hero meets a stranger who looks identical to him and who leads him into a long sequence of hideous crimes. "I was a being incomprehensible to myself. Either I had a second self, who transacted business in my likeness, or else my body was at times possessed by a spirit over which it had no control, and of those actions my own soul was wholly unconscious," wrote Robert Colwan, the hero of Hogg's novel. Whether Colwan's double is in fact a projection of his schizophrenic self or whether he is the devil himself is left for the reader to decide. Stevenson had read *The Justified Sinner* and admired it. The similarities between it and *Dr Jekyll and Mr Hyde* are striking. In both, the double is the expression of all the secret desires of the hero, those aspects of his personality which he had sought to suppress. Colwan, like Jekyll, is doomed. Once the double is acknowledged, he never rests until he is in control. And his dominance destroys them both. Here is a final extract from Dr Jekyll's letter. It takes up the story at the point where Dr Lanyon's description of the transformation back from Hyde to Jekyll left off.

(*g*)   When I came to myself at Lanyon's, the horror of my old friend perhaps affected me somewhat: I do not know; it was at least but a drop in the sea to the abhorrence with which I looked back upon these hours. A change had come over me. It was no longer the fear of the gallows, it was the horror of being Hyde that racked me. I received Lanyon's condemnation partly in a dream; it was partly in a dream that I came home to my own house and got into bed. I slept after the prostration of the day, with a stringent and profound slumber which not even the nightmares that wrung me could avail to break. I awoke in the morning shaken, weakened, but refreshed. I still hated and feared the thought of the brute that slept within me, and I had not of course forgotten the appalling dangers of the day before; but I was once more at home, in my own house and close to my drugs; and gratitude for my escape shone so strong in my soul that it almost rivalled the brightness of hope.

I was stepping leisurely across the court after breakfast, drinking the chill of the air with pleasure, when I was seized again with those indescribable sensations that heralded the change; and I had but the time to gain the shelter of my cabinet, before I was once again

III : M. *The horror of my other self. A drawing by S. G. Hulme Beaman in a 1930s edition of* Jekyll and Hyde. *Notice the emphasis on the surroundings and the patterns of light compared to the wraith-like Hyde. Is the other self a substantial being or a projection of Dr Jekyll's mind?*

raging and freezing with the passions of Hyde. It took on this occasion a double dose to recall me to myself; and alas! six hours after, as I sat looking sadly in the fire, the pangs returned, and the drug had to be readministered.

In short, from that day forth it seemed only by a great effort of gymnastics, and only under the immediate stimulation of the drug, that I was able to wear the countenance of Jekyll. At all hours of the day and night, I would be taken with the premonitory shudder; above all, if I slept, or even dozed for a moment in my chair, it was always as Hyde that I awakened. Under the strain of this continually

impending doom and by the sleeplessness to which I now con-
demned myself, ay, even beyond what I had thought possible to
man, I became, in my own person, a creature eaten up and emptied
by fever, languidly weak both in body and mind, and solely occupied
by one thought: the horror of my other self. But when I slept, or
when the virtue of the medicine wore off, I would leap almost
without transition (for the pangs of transformation grew daily less
marked) into the possession of a fancy brimming with images of
terror, a soul boiling with causeless hatreds, and a body that seemed
not strong enough to contain the raging energies of life.

The powers of Hyde seemed to have grown with the sickliness of
Jekyll. And certainly the hate that now divided them was equal on
each side. With Jekyll, it was a thing of vital instinct. He had now
seen the full deformity of that creature that shared with him some of
the phenomena of consciousness, and was co-heir with him to
death: and beyond these links of community, which in themselves
made the most poignant part of his distress, he thought of Hyde, for
all his energy of life, as of something not only hellish but inorganic.
This was the shocking thing; that the slime of the pit seemed to
utter cries and voices; that the amorphous dust gesticulated and
sinned; that what was dead, and had no shape, should usurp the
offices of life. And this again, that that insurgent horror was knit to
him closer than a wife, closer than an eye; lay caged in his flesh,
where he heard it mutter and felt it struggle to be born; and at
every hour of weakness, and in the confidence of slumber, prevailed
against him, and deposed him out of life.

The hatred of Hyde for Jekyll, was of a different order. His terror
of the gallows drove him continually to commit temporary suicide,
and return to his subordinate station of a part instead of a person;
but he loathed the necessity, he loathed the despondency into
which Jekyll was now fallen, and he resented the dislike with which
he was himself regarded. Hence the apelike tricks that he would
play me, scrawling in my own hand blasphemies on the pages of my
books, burning the letters and destroying the portrait of my father;
and indeed, had it not been for his fear of death, he would long ago
have ruined himself in order to involve me in the ruin. But this love
of life is wonderful; I go further: I, who sicken and freeze at the mere
thought of him, when I recall the abjection and passion of this
attachment, and when I know how he fears my power to cut him off
by suicide, I find it in my heart to pity him.

IV Dracula

1   "Sometimes the eyes were closed; more frequently open, glazed, fixed and glaring fiercely. The lips which will be markedly full and red are drawn back from the teeth which gleam long, sharp as razors and ivory white. Often the gaping mouth is stained and foul with great slab gouts of blood, which trickles down from the corners on to the lawn shroudings and linen cerements, the offal of the last night's feast. In the case of an epidemic of vampirism it is recorded that whole graves have been discovered soaked and saturated with squelching blood, which the horrid inhabitant has gorged until he is replete and vomited forth in great quantities like some swollen leech discharges when thrown into brine." That description was written by Rev. Montague Summers, an English clergyman with an overpowering interest in vampires. You probably noticed the sense of relishing the repugnant details which he is describing. There is simultaneously a feeling of repulsion and a feeling of fatal attraction. You could say that this chapter on *Dracula* is the first time that we come face to face with real horror. It is the *idea* of *Frankenstein* which is frightening, just as it is the *idea* of *Dr Jekyll and Mr Hyde*. But with *Dracula*, we are being invited to participate in all the *sensations* of horror. For the first time, we are having to accumulate loathsome details in order to understand the story.

2   Unlike *Frankenstein* and unlike *Jekyll and Hyde*, *Dracula* is one of a crowd. There are many different and quite independent vampires described in all sorts of novels, short stories, poems, plays and films. But because Dracula is the most famous, all the traditions about vampires have become attached to him. The other difference between Dracula and the previous characters we have looked at, is that, although he has as they had a precise fictional origin, there has been for a long time quite a widespread belief in the literal reality of vampires. Indeed, this belief still persists. Last year a man choked to death because he always insisted on sleeping with his mouth full of garlic to ward off vampires. Dracula, the grim Transylvanian count, is simply the most vivid consolidation of a vast body of superstitions, traditions and fears which already existed long before Bram Stoker ever put pen to paper.

3   Much is common popular knowledge now. Vampires, of course, drink human blood. They have long canine teeth, which they sink into the jugular veins of their victims, and then they suck out their blood. They can change into bats; they are active only at night; they hate crucifixes and garlic; the only way to be rid of them is to drive a stake through their hearts as they sleep in their coffins. Here is an extract from *Dracula* in which Van

IV : A. *Publicity poster for the most famous of Dracula films.*

Helsing, the old Dutch professor, explains the origins and the limits of the vampire's power.

(*a*)   "There are such beings as vampires; some of us have evidence that they exist. Even had we not the proof of our own unhappy experience, the teachings and the records of the past give proof enough for sane peoples. I admit that at the first I was sceptic. Were it not that through long years I have trained myself to keep an open mind, I could not have believed until such time as that fact thunder on my ear: 'See! see! I prove; I prove. Alas! Had I known at the first what now I know — nay, had I even guess at him — one so precious life had been spared to many of us who did love her. But that is gone; and we must so work that other poor souls perish not, whilst we can save. The *nosferatu* do not die like the bee when he sting once. He is only stronger; and being stronger, have yet more power to work evil.

This vampire which is amongst us is of himself so strong in person as twenty men; he is of cunning more than mortal, for his cunning be the growth of ages; he have still the aids of necromancy, which is, as his etymology imply, the divination by the dead, and all the dead that he can come nigh to are for him at command; he is brute, and more than brute; he is devil in callous, and the heart of him is not; he can, within limitations, appear at will when, and where, and in any of the forms that are to him; he can, within his range, direct the elements: the storm, the fog, the thunder; he can command all the meaner things: the rat, and the owl, and the bat — the moth, and the fox, and the wolf; he can grow and become small; and he can at times vanish and come unknown.

How then are we to begin our strife to destroy him? How shall we find his where; and having found it, how can we destroy? My friends, this is much; it is a terrible task that we undertake, and there may be consequence to make the brave shudder. For if we fail in this our fight he must surely win: and then where end we? Life is nothings! I heed him not. But to fail here is not mere life or death. It is that we become as him; that we henceforward become foul things of the night like him — without heart or conscience, preying on the bodies and the souls of those we love best. To us for ever are the gates of heaven shut; for who shall open them to us again? We go on for all time abhorred by all; a blot on the face of God's sunshine; an arrow in the side of Him who died for man. But we are face to face with duty; and in such case must we shrink? For me, I say, no; but then I am old, and life, with his sunshine, his fair places, his song of birds, his music, and his love, lie far behind. You others are young. Some have seen sorrow; but there are fair days yet in store. What say you?"

Whilst he was speaking Jonathan had taken my hand. I feared, oh so much, that the appalling nature of our danger was overcoming him when I saw his hand stretch out; but it was life to me to feel its touch — so strong, so self-reliant, so resolute. A brave man's hand can speak for itself; it does not even need a woman's love to hear its music.

When the Professor had done speaking my husband looked in my eyes, and I in his; there was no need for speaking between us.

"I answer for Mina and myself," he said.

"Count me in, Professor," said Mr Quincey Morris, laconically as usual.

"I am with you," said Lord Godalming, "for Lucy's sake, if for no other reason."

Dr Seward simply nodded. The Professor stood up, and, after laying his golden crucifix on the table, held out his hand on either side. I took his right hand, and Lord Godalming his left; Jonathan held my right with his left and stretched across to Mr Morris. So as we all took hands our solemn compact was made. I felt my heart icy cold, but it did not even occur to me to draw back. We resumed our places, and Dr Van Helsing went on with a sort of cheerfulness which showed that the serious work had begun. It was to be taken as gravely, and in as business-like a way, as any other transaction of life: —

"Well, you know what we have to contend against; but we, too, are not without strength. We have on our side power of combination – a power denied to the vampire kind; we have resources of science; we are free to act and think; and the hours of the day and the night are ours equally. In fact, so far as our powers extend, they are unfettered, and we are free to use them. We have self-devotion in a cause, and an end to achieve which is not a selfish one. These things are much.

"Now let us see how far the general powers arrayed against us are restrict, and how the individual cannot. In fine, let us consider the limitations of the vampire in general, and of this one in particular.

"All we have to go upon are traditions and superstitions. These do not at the first appear much, when the matter is one of life and death – nay, of more than either life or death. Yet must we be satisfied; in the first place because we have to be – no other means is at our control – and secondly, because, after all, these things – tradition and superstition – are everything. Does not the belief in vampires rest for others – though not, alas! for us – on them? A year ago which of us would have received such a possibility, in the midst of our scientific, sceptical, matter-of-fact nineteenth century? We even scouted a belief that we saw justified under our very eyes. Take it, then, that the vampire, and the belief in his limitations and his cure, rest for the moment on the same base.

For, let me tell you, he is known everywhere that men have been. In old Greece, in old Rome; he flourish in Germany all over, in France, in India, even in the Chersonese; and in China, so far from us in all ways, there even is he, and the peoples fear him at this day. He have follow the wake of the berserker Icelander, the devil-begotten Hun, the Slav, the Saxon, the Magyar. So far, then, we have all we may act upon; and let me tell you that very much of the beliefs are justified by what we have seen in our own so unhappy experience.

The vampire live on, and cannot die by mere passing of the time; he can flourish when that he can fatten on the blood of the living. Even more, we have seen amongst us that he can even grow younger; that his vital faculties grow strenuous, and seem as though they refresh themselves when his special pabulum is plenty. But he cannot flourish without this diet; he eat not as others. Even friend Jonathan, who lived with him for weeks, did never see him to eat, never! He throws no shadow; he make in the mirror no reflect, as again Jonathan observe. He has the strength of many in his hand – witness again Jonathan when he shut the door against the wolfs, and when he help him from the diligence too. He can transform himself to wolf, as we gather from the ship arrival in Whitby, when he tear open the dog; he can be as bat, as Madam Mina saw him on the window at Whitby, and as friend John saw him fly from this so near house, and as my friend Quincey saw him at the window of Miss Lucy. He can come in mist which he create – that noble ship's captain proved him of this; but, from what we know, the distance he can make this mist is limited, and it can only be round himself. He come on moonlight rays as elemental dust – as again Jonathan saw those sisters in the castle of Dracula. He become so small – we ourselves saw Miss Lucy, ere she was at peace, slip through a hair-breadth space at the tomb door. He can, when once he find his way, come out from anything or into anything, no matter how close it be bound or even fused up with fire – solder you call it. He can see in the dark – no small power this, in a world which is one half shut from the light.

Ah, but hear me through. He can do all these things, yet he is not

IV : B. *Roman Polanski staking a vampire in* Dance of the Vampires.

free. Nay, he is even more prisoner than the slave of the galley, than the madman in his cell. He cannot go where he lists; he who is not of nature has yet to obey some of nature's laws — why we know not. He may not enter anywhere at the first, unless there be someone of the household who bid him to come; though afterwards he can come as he please. His power ceases, as does that of all evil things, at the coming of the day. Only at certain times can he have limited freedom.

If he be not at the place whither he is bound, he can only change himself at noon or at exact sunrise or sunset. These things are we told, and in this record of ours we have proof by inference. Thus, whereas he can do as he will within his limit, when he have his earth-home, his coffin-home, his hell-home, the place unhallowed, as we saw when he went to the grave of the suicide at Whitby; still at other time he can only change when the time come. It is said, too, that he can only pass running water at the slack or the flood of the tide.

Then there are things which so afflict him that he has no power, as the garlic that we know of, and as for things sacred, as this symbol, my crucifix, that was amongst us even now when we resolve, to them he is nothing, but in their presence he take his place far off and silent with respect. There are others, too, which I shall tell you of, lest in our seeking we may need them. The branch of wild rose on his coffin keep him that he move not from it; a sacred bullet fired into the coffin kill him so that he be true dead; and as for the stake through him, we know already of its peace; or the cut-off head that giveth rest. We have seen it with our eyes."

4   Historically, there are two sources for the story of *Dracula*. The fifteenth-century Wallachian chieftain Vlad Drakula who impaled 23,000 victims to help the spread of Christianity and the seventeenth-century Countess Bathori who drank the blood of 650 young girls to preserve her youth, have become fused into a single character. There is also a tradition in Central Europe of peasant vampires (known as *vampyrs* or *vrykolakas*) and there was certainly in eighteenth-century Slovakia an outbreak of vampirism which reached epidemic proportions. Although many of these stories lack documentary proof and are probably exaggerated, there certainly are people who are so attracted by human blood that they behave in a way which is very similar to the vampire. As recently as 1949, a man called John George Haigh was convicted at the Old Baily and later hanged for murdering nine people. After he had killed each of them, he proceeded to drink quantities of their blood.

5   But the vampire legend has a much stronger and more basic hold over us than can be accounted for by factual references. At the centre of the encounter between vampire and victim are sadism and sexuality. In order to understand just how these elements combine, it is necessary first of all to think of *Dracula* in the context of the time when it was written. You must already have noticed how *Frankenstein*, which is, apart from anything else, the finest prose narrative work produced by the English Romantic movement, presented a highly idealized view of

IV : C. *Plate   from*   Les
Vampires *by Tony Faivre*
(Le Terrain Vague).

human relationships. Between the Romantics and the date of
composition of *Dracula* comes the Victorian age, when a most
virulent wave of sexual repression swept through the whole of
English culture and society. You have seen how *Jekyll and Hyde*
challenged the essentially hypocritical nature of the Victorian
façade of respectability, but in *Dracula* Bram Stoker strikes
deeply into the roots of the most pervasive area of prejudice,
namely that surrounding sex. It would, of course, be an oversim-
plification to see *Dracula* as a work of sexual liberation. All the
repressions and tensions of the Victorians are still present, but
as well as producing the long, rather strained passages about

sweetness, purity and nonspecific sanctity, they also generate a whole new area of sensational sexuality. To say that the encounter between the vampire and his victim is expressed erotically, is an indication of how the elements of fantasy within the myth serve to emphasize the preoccupations of the society.

6   It is precisely because sexuality had been so suppressed for so long that it emerges in *Dracula* in such a particular, even disguised form. It is another and much nastier form of the relationship between monster and victim which we looked at in *Frankenstein*. Now we are forced to consider the intense physicality of the encounter: the softness of the flesh, the sharpness of the teeth, the warmth of the blood. There is nothing to redeem the vampire. There is no high ideal gone wrong. He is evil, absolutely, and concerned only to gratify his own desires. That is why there is something much nastier about Dracula than about any of the other horror monsters. His is a myth of exploitation. The elements of sadism which pervade the relationship between the vampire and his victim are similarly part of the overlap between fantasy and reality. From a psychological point of view, sadism can be seen as a common factor in fantasies which offer an outlet to suppressed sexuality. At the same time, we are all to some extent predators or victims. The vampire myth converts into another and more extreme form our feelings about relationships between ordinary men and women. Through vampire stories, we can experience at second hand our fantasies of dominating or being dominated. Here cruelty and sexuality mean the same thing. There is no reason within the vampire legends why vampire and victim should be of different sexes, but almost invariably the male vampire has female victims and the female vampire male victims. Thus, our reality perception of relationships between people is being welded to a particular kind of fantasy, so that the myth which emerges is creating an alternative to any normative view. The following extract, from Sheridan Le Fanu's *Carmilla*, gives an impression of the extent to which something like a sexual encounter between two people has been skewed to accommodate the vampire.

(*b*)   Certain vague and strange sensations visited me in my sleep. The prevailing one was of that pleasant, peculiar cold thrill which we feel in bathing, when we move against the current of a river. This was soon accompanied by dreams that seemed interminable, and were so vague that I could never recollect their scenery and persons, or any one connected portion of their action. But they left an awful impression, and a sense of exhaustion, as If I had passed through a long period of great mental exertion and danger. After all these dreams there remained on waking a remembrance of having been in a place very nearly dark, and of having spoken to people whom I could not see; and especially of one clear voice, of a female's, very deep, that spoke as if at a distance, slowly, and producing always the same sensation of indescribable solemnity and fear. Sometimes there came a sensation as if a hand was drawn softly along my cheek and

IV : D. *The illustration to Chapter 1 of* Varney the Vampire.

neck. Sometimes it was as if warm lips kissed me, and longer and more lovingly as they reached my throat, but there the caress fixed itself. My heart beat faster, my breathing rose and fell rapidly and full drawn; a sobbing, that rose into a sense of strangulation, supervened, and turned into a dreadful convulsion, in which my senses left me, and I became unconscious.

7   You may remember (II : 2) that on the same occasion that Mary Shelley wrote *Frankenstein*, Lord Byron began a story called *The Vampyre*. He never finished it himself, but the idea was taken up by his friend Polidori, who completed the novel and published it in 1819. The vampire of the title is an English nobleman called Lord Ruthven, who is in many ways similar to Count Dracula. He became the most famous literary villain of his

time and, just as *Dracula* was later, the novel was successfully adapted for the stage. It was the start of quite a fashion in vampire stories, including the 800 pages of *Varney the Vampire* (1847) and culminating in *Dracula* which was written in 1897 by Bram Stoker. There can be little doubt that Stoker had already done some preliminary research before he started to write the book, but it is interesting that he attributes the actual birth of the story to a dream. Having eaten "too generous a helping of dressed crab at supper one night" he had a nightmare which gave him the idea for the story.

8   *Dracula* is the longest of the books we have looked at and has by far the most complicated story. Like *The Strange Case of Dr Jekyll and Mr Hyde*, it is written as if from several different points of view. There is no section of the book which is straight narrative. It is all in the form of diaries, letters, telegrams, even a kind of primitive tape-recording. The idea is to make the incredible events which are being described seem more real and easier to believe in. The story has far too many twists and turns and there are far too many characters for me to be able to summarize it as fully as I did *Jekyll and Hyde*. The central issue in the book is the removal of Count Dracula from his castle in Transylvania, where he seems to be rapidly running out of possible victims, to the densely populated and previously untapped city of London. Jonathan Harker, an English estate agent, visits Castle Dracula to complete negotiations about some property which Count Dracula is buying in London. He learns the awful truth about his host but is unable to prevent him migrating to England. Dracula arrives on a ship which is found with all its crewmen dead. In London, two girls, Lucy Westenra and Jonathan Harker's fiancée Mina Murray, become his victims. Meanwhile, Harker has returned from Transylvania and together with Dr Seward (a psychiatrist), Van Helsing (the Dutch professor) and two other men, sets out to rid the world of the evil Count. Under the leadership of Van Helsing, this intrepid band chase Dracula back to Transylvania where, at the last possible moment, he meets the traditional end of vampires, with a wooden stake driven through his heart, and Mina Murray is saved from a fate worse than death.

9   Much of the story suffers from the same kind of sentimentality and overplayed melodrama which characterizes many other Victorian novels of suspense. But there is certainly an imaginative power in the concept of Count Dracula, with his limitless resources for evil, which prevents the story becoming incredible or ridiculous. Here is Jonathan Harker's description of Dracula when he first meets him.

(*c*)   His face was a strong — a very strong — aquiline, with high bridge of the thin nose and peculiarly arched nostrils; with lofty domed forehead, and hair growing scantily round the temples, but profusely elsewhere. His eyebrows were very massive, almost meeting over the nose, and with bushy hair that seemed to curl in its own profusion. The mouth, so far as I could see it under the heavy moustache, was fixed and rather cruel-looking, with peculiarly sharp white teeth; these protruded over the lips, whose remarkable ruddiness showed astonishing vitality in a man of his years. For the rest, his ears were pale and at the tops extremely pointed; the chin was broad and strong, and the cheeks firm though thin. The general effect was one of extraordinary pallor.

10   Later, when he has been imprisoned by Dracula in the castle and he realizes that if he does not escape he will be killed, Harker searches in the hope of finding the key to the main gate. Eventually, he comes upon the coffin in the corner of the chapel where Dracula sleeps during the daylight hours.

(*d*)   The great box was in the same place, close against the wall, but the lid was laid on it, not fastened down, but with the nails ready in their places to be hammered home. I knew I must search the body for the key, so I raised the lid and laid it back against the wall; and then I saw something which filled my very soul with horror. There lay the Count, but looking as if his youth had been half-renewed, for the white hair and moustache were changed to dark iron-grey; the cheeks were fuller, and the white skin seemed ruby-red underneath; the mouth was redder than ever, for on the lips were gouts of fresh blood, which trickled from the corners of the mouth and ran over the chin and neck. Even the deep, burning eyes seemed set amongst swollen flesh, for the lids and pouches underneath were bloated. It seemed as if the whole awful creature were simply gorged with blood; he lay like a filthy leech, exhausted with his repletion.

I shuddered as I bent over to touch him, and every sense in me revolted at the contact; but I had to search, or I was lost. The coming night might see my own body a banquet in a similar way to those horrid three. I felt all over the body, but no sign could I find of the key. Then I stopped and looked at the Count. There was a mocking smile on the bloated face which seemed to drive me mad. This was the being I was helping to transfer to London, where, perhaps for centuries to come, he might, amongst its teeming millions, satiate his lust for blood, and create a new and ever widening circle of semi-demons to batten on the helpless.

The very thought drove me mad. A terrible desire came upon me to rid the world of such a monster. There was no lethal weapon at hand, but I seized a shovel which the workmen had been using to fill the cases, and lifting it high, struck, with the edge downward, at the hateful face. But as I did so the head turned, and the eyes fell full upon me, with all their blaze of basilisk horror. The sight seemed to paralyse me, and the shovel turned in my hand and glanced from the face, merely making a deep gash above the forehead. The shovel fell from my hand across the box, and as I pulled it away the flange of the blade caught the edge of the lid, which fell over again, and hid the horrid thing from my sight. The last glimpse I had was of the bloated face, bloodstained and fixed with a grin of malice which would have held its own in the nethermost hell.

11   Certainly, the most effective passages in the book occur in the opening section, which describes Harker's terrifying stay at Castle Dracula. The feeling of total isolation, the carefully created

atmosphere of gloom, despair and then sensuous evil, these are used by Stoker to create an impression of horror which is never equalled later, even in the most lurid sections of the events in London. It is Transylvania which has become associated in people's minds with Dracula and although it occupies only about an eighth of the book, it is by far the most vivid and memorable. In London, we are sure that everything will be bound to turn out for the best in the end. But in Transylvania, we can comfort ourselves with no such easy assurances. Harker is the heroic victim in a whole world of evil; while in London, Dracula, however powerful, soon becomes the hunted as well as the hunter, the sacrifice as well as the high priest. Here is an early section in which Harker, who has been exploring Castle Dracula, does not heed the Count's warning to return before nightfall to his own room.

(e)   I was not alone. The room was the same, unchanged in any way since I came into it; I could see along the floor, in the brilliant moonlight, my own footsteps marked where I had disturbed the long accumulation of dust. In the moonlight opposite me were three young women, ladies by their dress and manner. I thought at the time that I must be dreaming when I saw them, for, though the moonlight was behind them, they threw no shadow on the floor.

They came close to me and looked at me for some time and then whispered together. Two were dark, and had high aquiline noses, like the Count's, and great dark, piercing eyes, that seemed to be almost red when contrasted with the pale yellow moon. The other was fair, as fair as can be, with great, wavy masses of golden hair and eyes like pale sapphires. I seemed somehow to know her face, and to know it in connection with some dreamy fear, but I could not recollect at the moment how or where. All three had brilliant white teeth, that shone like pearls against the ruby of their voluptuous lips.

There was something about them that made me uneasy, some longing and at the same time some deadly fear. I felt in my heart a wicked, burning desire that they would kiss me with those red lips. It is not good to note this down, lest some day it should meet Mina's eyes and cause her pain; but it is the truth. They whispered together, and then they all three laughed — such a silvery, musical laugh, but as hard as though the sound never could have come through the softness of human lips. It was like the intolerable, tingling sweetness of water-glasses when played on by a cunning hand. The fair girl shook her head coquettishly, and the other two urged her on. One said: —

"Go on! You are first, and we shall follow; yours is the right to begin." The other added: —

"He is young and strong; there are kisses for us all." I lay quiet, looking out under my eyelashes in an agony of delightful anticipation. The fair girl advanced and bent over me till I could feel the movement of her breath upon me. Sweet it was in one sense, honey-sweet, and sent the same tingling through the nerves as her voice, but with a bitter underlying the sweet, a bitter offensiveness, as one smells in blood.

I was afraid to raise my eyelids, but looked out and saw perfectly under the lashes. The fair girl went on her knees and bent over me, fairly gloating. There was a deliberate voluptuousness which was

IV:E. *From Vampirella, a sequence from a typical vampire strip, heavily influenced by Dracula.*

59

IV : F. *The scene with the three female vampires from the Bela Lugosi Dracula.*

both thrilling and repulsive, and as she arched her neck she actually licked her lips like an animal, till I could see in the moonlight the moisture shining on the scarlet lips and on the red tongue as it lapped the white sharp teet. Lower and lower went her head as the lips went below the range of my mouth and chin and seemed about to fasten on my throat. Then she paused, and I could hear the churning sound of her tongue as it licked her teeth and lips, and could feel the hot breath on my neck. Then the skin of my throat began to tingle as one's flesh does when the hand that is to tickle it approaches nearer — nearer. I could feel the soft, shivering touch of the lips on the supersensitive skin of my throat, and the hard dents of two sharp teeth, just touching and pausing there. I closed my eyes in a languorous ecstasy and waited — waited with beating heart.

But at that instant another sensation swept through me as quick as lightning. I was conscious of the presence of the Count, and of his being as if lapped in a storm of fury. As my eyes opened involuntarily I saw his strong hand grasp the slender neck of the fair woman and with giant's power draw it back, the blue eyes transformed with fury, the white teeth champing with rage, and the fair cheeks blazing red with passion. But the Count! Never did I imagine such wrath and fury, even in the demons of the pit. His eyes were positively blazing. The red light in them was lurid, as if the flames of hell-fire blazed behind them. His face was deathly pale, and the lines of it were hard like drawn wires; the thick eyebrows that met over the nose now seemed like a heaving bar of white-hot metal. With a fierce sweep of his arm, he hurled the woman from him, and then motioned to the others, as though he were beating them back; it was the same imperious gesture that I had seen used to the wolves. In a voice which, though low and almost a whisper, seemed to cut through the air and then ring round the room, he exclaimed: —

"How dare you touch him, any of you? How dare you cast eyes on him when I had forbidden it? Back, I tell you all! This man belongs to me! Beware how you meddle with him, or you'll have to deal with me." The fair girl, with a laugh of ribald coquetry, turned to answer him: —

"You yourself never loved; you never love!" On this the other women joined, and such a mirthless, hard, soulless laughter rang through the room that it almost made me faint to hear; it seemed like the pleasure of fiends. Then the Count turned, after looking at my face attentively, and said in a soft whisper: —

"Yes, I too can love; you yourselves can tell it from the past. Is it not so? Well, now I promise you that when I am done with him, you shall kiss him at your will. Now go! go! I must awaken him, for there is work to be done."

"Are we to have nothing to–night?" said one of them, with a low laugh, as she pointed to the bag which he had thrown upon the floor, and which moved as though there were some living thing within it. For answer he nodded his head. One of the women jumped forward and opened it. If my ears did not deceive me there was a gasp and a low wail, as of a half-smothered child. The women closed round, whilst I was aghast with horror; but as I looked they disappeared, and with them the dreadful bag. There was no door near them, and they could not have passed me without my noticing. They simply seemed to fade into the rays of the moonlight and pass out through the window, for I could see outside the dim, shadowy forms for a moment before they entirely faded away.

Then the horror overcame me, and I sank down unconscious.

12   Visually, of course, it is the Transylvanian sections of *Dracula* which convert most effectively into films. The possibilities for gloomy atmospheric sets with castles, forests and ancestral tombs are endless. The audience is frightened not by the unexpected, but because they *do* know exactly what is going to happen. The fear is not in the surprise, but in anticipating the inevitable chain of events. That is why *Dracula*, like *Frankenstein* and *Dr Jekyll and Mr Hyde*, is a modern myth. It is a world full of awful possibilities and meanings, but it is also a world in which nothing can ever change.

13   The first Dracula film to be made was based very closely on Stoker's novel, but in order to evade the copyright law, the names of the characters and the location of the action were changed. The film was called *Nosferatu* and was made by F. W. Murnau in 1921. Only the ending departs significantly from the book. The vampire, lingering too long at the bedside of the

IV : G. *Max Schreck in* Nosferatu.

heroine, is killed by the first rays of the rising sun and his body simply dissolves away. Ten years later, the Danish director Carl Dreyer made *Vampyr*, which is a mysterious, extraordinarily atmospheric film, loosely based on *Carmilla* by Sheridan Le Fanu. It is not really the plot which is interesting. It is Dreyer's insistence that what matters are the right *sensations*. It is the knowledge of vampirism which creates the terror, not just the sharp teeth in the night. Dreyer shot the entire film through a piece of gauze to create the effect of a dreamlike and intangible evil. Here is how he described what he wanted to achieve: "Imagine that we are sitting in an ordinary room. Suddenly we are told that there is a corpse behind the door. In an instant the room we are sitting in is completely altered; everything in it has taken on another look: the light, the atmosphere have changed, though they are physically the same. This is because *we* have changed and the objects *are* as we conceive them. This is the effect I want to get in my film."

14 In the same year as *Vampyr*, the American company Universal released what is probably the best-known film of *Dracula* directed by Tod Browning and starring Bela Lugosi. Because the script was based on the stage play of *Dracula* rather than on the novel, the film is in places much too wordy and static. But Lugosi *is* Dracula and his total identification with the part enables him to project his evil presence throughout the film. The cold, sadistic power of Dracula is more evident in Lugosi's performance than in any other actor who has played the part, even Christopher Lee. There was, as might be expected, a series of follow-up films, various *Sons, Daughters, Brides, Returns* and *Scars of Dracula*, made principally in the thirties in America and in the sixties by Hammer Films in England.

15 It seems that the fatal fascination of *Dracula* persists. To account for his popularity, we must look further than sadism and sexuality. There are other, related aspects of the vampire phenomenon which contribute to its effect upon us. They are important because they are forbidden and thus the myth serves the function of letting us experience some basic but anti-social cravings. The first of these is *cannibalism*. The vampire sucks the blood, not of animals, but of people. "The life of the flesh is the blood," says Leviticus. The Christian tradition of the Last Supper, in which the faithful eat the body and drink the blood of Christ, their God, is the most obvious example of a form of sanctioned symbolic cannibalism. Many primitive cultures believe that by drinking the blood of your vanquished enemy, you add his strength to your own. This is related to the general idea of *sacrifice*, which involves killing some living thing as an offering to the god. In vampirism, of course, the high priest who offers the sacrifice of the victim is offering it to himself.

16 Another aspect of vampirism which is important in this forbidden way is *necrophilia*, which means love of death or dead people. There is always a feeling in *Dracula* of what Dreyer called "a corpse behind the door". In fact, our fascination with the encounter between the vampire and his victim can be seen as a kind of *death wish*, in which we surrender our wills in order to experience the sensations of death without the danger of actually dying. Vampires, of course, are un-dead. That is to say, they have died but they still continue to exist. They differ from

63

The Bela Lugosi Journal

THE OFFICIAL PUBLICATION OF THE AMERICAN BELA LUGOSI FAN CLUB

Vol. 1 — No. 1   48   CLEVELAND, OHIO   SUMMER - FALL, 1961

Special

MEMORIAL ISSUE

BIG MOVIE REVUE ON:

THE
BLACK CAT

(((●)))

BELA LUGOSI

MASTERY TEST

(((●)))

SPECIAL

CONTEST
REPORT

BELA LUGOSI as seen in the 1931 Universal thriller as Count Dracula

IV : H. *Following the success of* Dracula*, Bela Lugosi became the most popular movie star in America. The sex appeal of the vampire works both ways.*

what are often called the walking dead, in that they are not zombies, but self-determining and especially cunning. *Dracula*, like other vampire stories, is full of scenes set in tombs and churchyards. Here is quite a long scene in which the vampire hunters are preparing to dispose of Lucy, who, as one of Dracula's victims, has herself turned vampire. Arthur, who was Lucy's fiancé, still has his doubts about the whole plan.

(f)   It was just a quarter before twelve o'clock when we got into the churchyard over the low wall. The night was dark, with occasional gleams of moonlight between the rents of the heavy clouds that scudded across the sky. We all kept somehow close together, with Van Helsing slightly in front as he led the way. When we had come close to the tomb I looked well at Arthur, for I feared that the proximity to a place laden with so sorrowful a memory would upset him; but he bore himself well. I took it that the very mystery of the proceeding tended in some way to counteract his grief. The Professor unlocked the door, and seeing a natural hesitation amongst us for various reasons, solved the difficulty by entering first himself. The rest of us followed, and he closed the door. He then lit a dark lantern and pointed to the coffin. Arthur stepped forward hesitatingly; Van Helsing said to me: –

"You were with me here yesterday. Was the body of Miss Lucy in that coffin?"

"It was." The Professor turned to the rest, saying: –

"You hear; and yet there is one who does not believe with me."
He took his screwdriver and again took off the lid of the coffin. Arthur looked on, very pale but silent; when the lid was removed he stepped forward. He evidently did not know that there was a leaden coffin, or, at any rate, had not thought of it. When he saw the rent in the lead, the blood rushed to his face for an instant, but as quickly fell away again, so that he remained of a ghastly whiteness; he was still silent. Van Helsing forced back the leaden flange, and we all looked in and recoiled.

The coffin was empty!

For several minutes no one spoke a word. The silence was broken by Quincey Morris: –

"Professor, I answered for you. Your word is all I want. I wouldn't ask such a thing ordinarily – I wouldn't so dishonour you as to imply a doubt; but this is a mystery that goes beyond any honour or dishonour. Is this your doing?"

"I swear to you by all that I hold sacred that I have not removed nor touched her. What happened was this: Two nights ago my friend Seward and I came here – with good purpose, believe me. I opened that coffin, which was then sealed up, and we found it, as now, empty. We then waited, and saw something white come through the trees. The next day we came here in daytime, and she lay there. Did she not, friend John?"

"Yes."

"That night we were just in time. One more so small child was missing, and we find it, thank God, unharmed amongst the graves. Yesterday I came here before sundown, for at sundown the Un-Dead can move. I waited here all the night till the sun rose, but I saw nothing. It was most probable that it was because I had laid over the clamps of those doors garlic, which the Un-Dead cannot bear, and other things which they shun. Last night there was no exodus, so to-night before the sundown I took away my garlic and other things. And so it is we find this coffin empty. But bear with me. So far there is much that is strange. Wait you with me outside, unseen and unheard, and things much stranger are yet to be. So" — here he shut the dark slide of his lantern — "now to the outside." He opened the door, and we filed out, he coming last and locking the door behind him.

Oh! but it seemed fresh and pure in the night air after the terror of that vault. How sweet it was to see the clouds race by, and the brief gleams of the moonlight between the scudding clouds crossing and passing — like the gladness and sorrow of a man's life; how sweet it was to breathe the fresh air, that had no taint of death and decay; how humanising to see the red lighting of the sky beyond the hill, and to hear far away the muffled roar that marks the life of a great city. Each in his own way was solemn and overcome.

Arthur was silent, and was, I could see, striving to grasp the purpose and the inner meaning of the mystery. I was myself tolerably patient, and half inclined again to throw aside doubt and to accept Van Helsing's conclusions. Quincey Morris was phlegmatic in the way of a man who accepts all things, and accepts them in the spirit of cool bravery, with hazard of all he has to stake. Not being able to smoke, he cut himself a good-sized plug of tobacco and began to chew. As to Van Helsing, he was employed in a definite way. First he took from his bag a mass of what looked like thin, wafer-like biscuit, which was carefully rolled up in a white napkin; next he took out a double-handful of some whitish stuff, like dough or putty. He crumbled the wafer up fine and worked it into the mass between his hands. This he then took, and rolling it into thin strips, began to lay them into the crevices between the door and its setting in the tomb. I was somewhat puzzled at this, and being close, asked him what it was that he was doing. Arthur and Quincey drew near also, as they too were curious. He answered: —

"I am closing the tomb, so that the Un-Dead may not enter."

"And is that stuff you have put there going to do it?" asked Quincey. "Great Scott! Is this a game?"

"It is."

"What is that which you are using?" This time the question was by Arthur. Van Helsing reverently lifted his hat as he answered: —

"The Host. I brought it from Amsterdam. I have an Indulgence." It was an answer that appalled the most sceptical of us, and we felt individually that in the presence of such earnest purpose as the Professor's, a purpose which could thus use the to him most sacred of things, it was impossible to distrust. In respectful silence we took the places assigned to us close round the tomb, but hidden from the sight of anyone approaching. I pitied the others, especially Arthur. I had myself been apprenticed by my former visits to this watching horror; and yet I, who had up to an hour ago repudiated the proofs, felt my heart sink within me. Never did tombs look so ghastly white; never did cypress, or yew, or juniper so seem the embodiment of funereal gloom; never did tree or grass wave or rustle so ominously; never did bough creak so mysteriously; and never did the far-away howling of dogs send such a woeful presage through the night.

There was a long spell of silence, a big, aching void, and then from the Professor a keen "S-s-s-s!" He pointed; and far down the avenue of yews we saw a white figure advance — a dim white figure, which held something dark at its breast. The figure stopped, and at the moment a ray of moonlight fell between the masses of driving clouds and showed in startling prominence a dark-haired woman, dressed in the cerements of the grave. We could not see the face, for it was bent down over what we saw to be a fair-haired child. There was a pause and a sharp little cry, such as a child gives in sleep, or a dog as it lies before the fire and dreams. We were starting forward, but the Professor's warning hand, seen by us as he stood behind a yew-tree, kept us back; and then as we looked the white figure moved forward again. It was now near enough for us to see clearly, and the moonlight still held. My own heart grew cold as ice, and I could hear the gasp of Arthur as we recognized the features of Lucy Westenra. Lucy Westenra, but yet how changed. The sweetness was turned to adamantine, heartless cruelty, and the purity to voluptuous wantonness. Van Helsing stepped out, and, obedient to his gesture, we all advanced too; the four of us ranged in a line before the door of the tomb. Van Helsing raised his lantern and drew the slide; by the concentrated light that fell on Lucy's face we could see that the lips were crimson with fresh blood, and that the stream had trickled over her chin and stained the purity of her lawn death-robe.

We shuddered with horror. I could see by the tremulous light that even Van Helsing's iron nerve had failed. Arthur was next to me, and if I had not seized his arm and held him up, he would have fallen.

When Lucy — I call the thing that was before us Lucy because it bore her shape — saw us she drew back with an angry snarl, such as a cat gives when taken unawares; then her eyes ranged over us. Lucy's eyes in form and colour; but Lucy's eyes unclean and full of hell-fire, instead of the pure, gentle orbs we knew. At that moment the remnant of my love passed into hate and loathing; had she then to be killed, I could have done it with savage delight. As she looked, her eyes blazed with unholy light, and the face became wreathed with a voluptuous smile. Oh, God, how it made me shudder to see it! With a careless motion, she flung to the ground, callous as a devil, the child that up to now she had clutched strenuously to her breast, growling over it as a dog growls over a bone. The child gave a sharp cry, and lay there moaning. There was a cold-bloodedness in the act which wrung a groan from Arthur; when she advanced to him with outstretched arms and a wanton smile, he fell back and hid his face in his hands.

She still advanced, however, and with a languorous, voluptuous grace, said: —

"Come to me, Arthur. Leave these others and come to me. My arms are hungry for you. Come, and we can rest together. Come, my husband, come!"

There was something diabolically sweet in her tones — something of the tingling of glass when struck — which rang through the brains even of us who heard the words addressed to another. As for Arthur, he seemed under a spell; moving his hands from his face, he opened wide his arms. She was leaping for them, when Van Helsing spring forward and held between them his little golden crucifix. She recoiled from it, and, with a suddenly distorted face, full of rage, dashed past him as if to enter the tomb.

When within a foot or two of the door, however, she stopped as if arrested by some irresistible force. Then she turned, and her face was shown in the clear burst of moonlight and by the lamp, which had now no quiver from Van Helsing's iron nerves. Never did I see such baffled malice on a face; and never, I trust, shall such ever be seen again by mortal eyes. The beautiful colour became vivid, the eyes seemed to throw out sparks of hellfire, the brows were wrinkled as though the folds of the flesh were the coils of Medusa's snakes, and the lovely, blood-stained mouth grew to an open square, as in the passion masks of the Greeks and Japanese. If ever a face meant death — if looks could kill — we saw it at that moment.

IV : J. *Sandra Harrison in* Blood of
Dracula.

She enters the tomb. They return the next day to complete
their task.

When we were alone and had heard the last of the footsteps die
out up the road, we silently, and as if by ordered intention, followed
the Professor to the tomb. He unlocked the door, and we entered,
closing it behind us. Then he took from his bag the lantern, which he

lit, and also two wax candles, which, when lighted, he stuck, by melting their own ends, on other coffins, so that they might give light sufficient to work by. When he again lifted the lid off Lucy's coffin we all looked — Arthur trembling like an aspen — and saw that the body lay there in all its death-beauty. But there was no love in my own heart, nothing but loathing for the foul Thing which had taken Lucy's shape without her soul. I could see even Arthur's face grow hard as he looked. Presently he said to Van Helsing: —

"Is this really Lucy's body, or only a demon in her shape?"

"It is her body, and yet not it. But wait a while, and you shall see her as she was, and is."

She seemed like a nightmare of Lucy as she lay there; the pointed teeth, the bloodstained, voluptuous mouth — which it made one shudder to see — the whole carnal and unspiritual appearance, seeming like a devilish mockery of Lucy's sweet purity. Van Helsing, in his methodical manner, began taking the various contents from his bag and placing them ready for use. First he took out a soldering iron and some plumbing solder, and then a small oil-lamp, which gave out, when lit in a corner of the tomb, gas which burned at fierce heat with a blue flame; then his operating knives, which he placed to hand; and last a round wooden stake, some two and a half or three inches thick and about three feet long. One end of it was hardened by charring in the fire, and was sharpened to a fine point.

With this stake came a heavy hammer, such as in households is used in the coal-cellar for breaking the lumps. To me, a doctor's preparations for work of any kind are stimulating and bracing, but the effect of these things on both Arthur and Quincey was to cause them a sort of consternation. They both, however, kept their courage, and remained silent and quiet.

When all was ready, Van Helsing said: —

"Before we do anything, let me tell you this; it is out of the lore and experience of the ancients and of all those who have studied the powers of the Un-Dead. When they become such, there comes with the change the curse of immortality; they cannot die, but must go on age after age adding new victims and multiplying the evils of the world; for all that die from the preying of the Un-Dead become themselves Un-Dead, and prey on their kind. And so the circle goes on ever widening, like as the ripples from a stone thrown in the water. Friend Arthur, if you had met that kiss which you know of before poor Lucy die; or again, last night when you open your arms to her, you would in time, when you had died, have become *nosferatu*, as they call it in Eastern Europe, and would all time make more of those Un-Deads that so have filled us with horror.

The career of this so unhappy dear lady is but just begun. Those children whose blood she suck are not as yet so much the worse; but if she live on, Un-Dead, more and more they lose their blood, and by her power over them they come to her; and so she draw their blood with that so wicked mouth. But if she die in truth, then all cease; the tiny wounds of the throats disappear, and they go back to their plays unknowing ever of what has been. But of the most blessed of all, when this now Un-Dead be made to rest as true dead, then the soul of the poor lady whom we love shall again be free. Instead of working wickedness by night and growing more debased in the assimilation of it by day, she shall take her place with the other Angels. So that, my friend, it will be a blessed hand for her that shall strike the blow that sets her free. To this I am willing; but is there none amongst us who has a better right? Will it be no joy to think of hereafter in the silence of the night when sleep is not; 'It was my hand that sent her to the stars; it was the hand of him that loved her best; the hand that of all she would herself have chosen, had it been to her to choose'? Tell me if there be such a one amongst us."

We all looked at Arthur. He saw, too, what we all did, the infinite kindness which suggested that his should be the hand which would restore Lucy to us as a holy, and not an unholy, memory; he stepped forward and said bravely, though his hand trembled, and his face was as pale as snow: –

"My true friend, from the bottom of my broken heart I thank you. Tell me what I am to do, and I shall not falter!" Van Helsing laid a hand on his shoulder, and said: –

"Brave lad! A moment's courage, and it is done. This stake must be driven through her. It will be a fearful ordeal – be not deceived in that – but it will be only a short time, and you will then rejoice more than your pain was great; from this grim tomb you will emerge as though you tread on air. But you must not falter when once you have begun. Only think that we, your true friends, are round you, and that we pray for you all the time."

"Go on," said Arthur hoarsely. "Tell me what I am to do."

"Take this stake in your left hand, ready to place the point over the heart, and the hammer in your right. Then when we begin our prayer for the dead – I shall read him. I have here the book, and the others shall follow – strike in God's name, that so all may be well with the dead that we love, and that the Un-Dead pass away."

Arthur took the stake and the hammer, and when once his mind was set on action his hands never trembled nor even quivered. Van Helsing opened his missal and began to read, and Quincey and I followed as well as we could. Arthur placed the point over the heart, and as I looked I could see its dint in the white flesh. Then he struck with all his might.

The Thing in the coffin writhed; and a hideous, blood-curdling screech came from the opened red lips. The body shook and quivered and twisted in wild contortions; the sharp white teeth champed together till the lips were cut and the mouth was smeared with a crimson foam. But Arthur never faltered. He looked like a figure of Thor as his untrembling arm rose and fell, driving deeper and deeper the mercy-bearing stake, whilst the blood from the pierced heart welled and spurted up around it. His face was set, and high duty seemed to shine through it; the sight of it gave us courage, so that our voices seemed to ring through the little vault.

And then the writhing and quivering of the body became less, and the teeth ceased to champ, and the face to quiver. Finally it lay still. The terrible task was over.

The hammer fell from Arthur's hand. He reeled and would have fallen had we not caught him. Great drops of sweat sprang out on his forehead, and his breath came in broken gasps. It had been an awful strain on him; and had he not been forced to his task by more than human considerations he could never have gone through with it. For a few minutes we were so taken up with him that we did not look towards the coffin. When we did, however, a murmur of startled surprise ran from one to the other of us. We gazed so eagerly that Arthur rose, for he had been seated on the ground, and came and looked too; and then a glad, strange light broke over his face and dispelled altogether the gloom of horror that lay upon it.

There in the coffin lay no longer the foul Thing that we had so dreaded and grown to hate that the work of her destruction was yielded as a privilege to the one best entitled to it, but Lucy as we had seen her in her life, with her face of unequalled sweetness and purity. True that there were there, as we had seen them in life, the

IV:K. *From* Carmilla. *Both vampire and victim are female. The possible bisexuality of the encounter
becomes explicit.*

traces of care and pain and waste; but these were all dear to us, for
they marked her truth to what we knew. One and all we felt that the
holy calm that lay like sunshine over the wasted face and form was
only an earthly token and symbol of the calm that was to reign for
ever.

17   This necrophilia becomes strongest when it is most closely
associated with the intense sexuality which, as we have already
seen, is an essential part of the sensation of horror which the
myth seeks to create. Here is an extract from a short story *The
Death of Ilalotha* by Clark Ashton Smith. Xantlicha is a queen,
Thulos is her husband and Ilalotha is a previous mistress of his
who has just died. He has gone to her tomb and Xantlicha has
followed him. In this extract, necrophilia and cannibalism are
taken so far that our natural fascination with the fact of death
leads to participation in an orgy where death is destroying life.

(g)   A few paces more, and Xantlicha stood as if a demon's arm had
arrested her: for her lanthorn's light had found the inverted face and
upper body of Thulos, hanging from the end of a burnished, new-
wrought sarcophagus that occupied a scant interval between others
green with rust. One of Thulos' hands clutched rigidly the rim of the
sarcophagus, while the other hand, moving feebly, seemed to caress
a dim shape that leaned above him with arms showing jasmine-
white in the narrow beam, and dark fingers plunging into his bosom.
His head and body seemed but an empty hull, and his hand hung
skeleton-thin on the bronze rim, and his whole aspect was vein-

71

drawn, as if he had lost more blood than was evident on his torn throat and face, and in his sodden raiment and dripping hair.

From the thing stooping above Thulos, there came ceaselessly that sound which was half moan and half snarl. And as Xantlicha stood in petrific fear and loathing, she seemed to hear from Thulos' lips an indistinct murmur, more of ecstasy than pain. The murmur ceased, and his head hung slacklier than before, so that the queen deemed him verily dead. At this she found such wrathful courage as enabled her to step nearer and raise the lanthorn higher: for, even amid her extreme panic, it came to her that by means of the wizard-poisoned dagger she might still haply slay the thing that had slain Thulos.

Waveringly the light crept aloft, disclosing inch by inch that infamy which Thulos had caressed in the darkness.

. . . It crept even to the crimson-smeared wattles, and the fanged and ruddled orifice that was half mouth and half beak . . . till Xantlicha knew why the body of Thulos was a mere shrunken hull. . . . In what the queen saw, there remained nothing of Ilalotha except the white, voluptuous arms, and a vague outline of human breasts melting momently into breasts that were not human, like clay moulded by a demon sculptor. The arms too began to change and darken; and, as they changed, the dying hand of Thulos stirred again and fumbled with a caressing movement toward the horror. And the thing seemed to heed him not but withdrew its fingers from his bosom, and reached across him with members stretching enormously, as if to claw the queen or fondle her with its dribbling talons.

It was then that Xantlicha let fall the lanthorn and the dagger, and ran with shrill, endless shriekings and laughters of immitigable madness from the vault.

18   Certainly Dracula is the nastiest of the horror monsters. He is perhaps the product of our fear of the unknown beyond us, while the others are the product of our fear of the unknown within ourselves.

V Conclusion

1   Of course, the stories of Frankenstein, Dr Jekyll and Mr Hyde, and Dracula are not the only stories of horror monsters. They are not even necessarily the only horror monsters which could be called modern myths. I can think of at least four other possibilities for inclusion, though none of them seems to me to have the popular and imaginative power of those we have already looked at. Quasimodo, or *The Hunchback of Notre Dame*, based on the novel by Victor Hugo, still has a certain power and currency, particularly as played by Charles Laughton in the 1939 film version, but little attention has been paid to the story since the war. *King Kong*, on the other hand, seems to be undergoing some kind of revival at present. He was the giant gorilla who

V : A. *King Kong.*

terrorized New York and, in true Beauty and the Beast tradition, is only conquered because of his soft spot for Fay Wray. The Beauty and the Beast theme is also apparent in *The Phantom of the Opera*, which is based on a novel by Gaston Leroux, and has been filmed three times. The only other possible mythic character is the more general figure of the *Werewolf*, who has featured in many books and films, but who is more of a type than a character and does not have a particular champion in the sense that Dracula is the champion of vampires.

2   The term modern myth is, in any case, only descriptive. It describes the *effect* that a story of character has had, rather than saying anything about the *intention* of whoever created it. Probably the most important issue which is raised by this book is why it is that horror monsters should occupy such a prominent place in our modern mythology.

V:B. *Lon Chaney as the Phantom of the Opera.*

VI Discussions

Frankenstein

1   Look at the pictures of the monsters in Chapter II. Do you notice any changes in the way people view him? The first known engraving (II : B) certainly shows a different kind of monster to Boris Karloff. Why do you think this change has taken place? Are we more difficult to shock nowadays? Must a monster *look* horrible to *be* horrible?

2   Because Frankenstein has created the monster, does that, as he assumes, give him the right to destroy him?

3   Frankenstein used parts of dead bodies to construct the monster. Nowadays, an increasing proportion of surgery is concerned with using organs from animals or human donors to replace defective organs in patients. This is known as spare-part surgery. Would it be possible one day to build a whole new person from spare parts? If so, need it be a monster? If this kind of surgery progresses, will surgeons become merely fitters rather than mechanics? If you had a brain transplant, who would you be after the operation?

4   Can you think of other examples of people who have been driven to terrorism and murder through being rejected and misunderstood by the society they live in? How much sympathy do you feel for these people? Do you think their extremist behaviour can be justified?

5   Do you think that the idea of the noble savage (II : 5) has any relevance to the world today?

Dr Jekyll and Mr Hyde

1   If you had to choose either Dr Jekyll or Mr Hyde to be your only companion, which would you prefer if you were (a) marooned on a desert island, (b) visiting Hong Kong for a fortnight, (c) going to a party, (d) going to church?

2   In his letter to Mr Utterson, Dr Jekyll writes about the mixture which transforms him into Mr Hyde: "The drug had no discriminating action; it was neither diabolical nor divine." What exactly does that mean? Do you agree with it? Is it true of all drugs, even those to which people become addicted? And what about the impulse that drives people to take the drug in the first place, is that also neither diabolical nor divine?

3   Even everyday drugs like alcohol sometimes make people act in ways which are not typical of their normal behaviour. A drunken driver is a kind of Mr Hyde. Is it right that the sober person should be held responsible for what the drunken person did?

4   The idea of taking a drug in order to bring about the transformation from Jekyll into Hyde has often been criticized as rather a crude way of describing how one person can have very different impulses and desires. I explained (III : 18) how an extreme form of this different behaviour is called schizophrenia. You have probably already discussed whether somebody under the influence of drink or drugs should be held responsible for his actions. But do you think that somebody who doctors agree is mad should be held responsible for his actions? If not, what sort of place is there for him in society?

5   A famous psychiatrist called R. D. Laing wrote in his book *The Divided Self*: "I am aware that the man who is said to be deluded may be in his delusion telling me the truth, and this in no equivocal or metaphorical sense, but quite literally, and that the cracked mind of the schizophrenic may *let in* light which does not enter the intact minds of many sane people whose minds are closed." This is a very difficult statement and it is one which many other psychiatrists have disagreed with. What do you think he means? Do you agree with him in any way at all?

Dracula

1   Many people *do* still believe in vampires (IV : 2) although it is clearly not reasonable to do so. Do you think that any particular kind of person is particularly liable to believe in vampires? Can such a belief be justified in any way?

2   Why is Dracula, like most other vampires, an aristocrat?

3   When a vampire sucks somebody's blood until they die, the victim also becomes a vampire after death. This is a form of reproduction of the un-dead. How do you think this relates to the idea of the death wish mentioned in IV : 16?

4   There have been many cases where people marooned on a barren island or in a lifeboat or trapped in a cave have chosen to eat one of their own number rather than all starve to death. Do you think this is morally wrong? Could you do it yourself? Or could you volunteer to be the one who was eaten?

5   An American writer has published a short story in which the vampire will drink only menstrual blood. Do you think that the idea is too disgusting to be effective? What exactly is it that makes some things seem more disgusting than others? Is everybody disgusted by the same things?

General

1   Which of the three characters we have looked at do you think is the most frightening, and why?

2   Which of the three characters we have looked at do you think is the most important as having a special meaning for us and the

way we live today? Was it the same one as you thought was most frightening?

3   Look at VI : A — Natural monsters. To what extent are we prepared to tolerate people who are different? Is the monster always the real victim?

4   Often you talk about the *moral* of a book. Do the three books we have looked at have morals? What are they? Are they three forms of the same moral or is there any important difference between them?

5   All three stories apparently had their origins in dreams which came to Mary Shelley (II : 3), Stevenson (III : 5) and Bram Stoker (IV : 7). Do you think this is just a coincidence or is there some special reason why these stories have this in common? Are dreams important, anyway? Have you ever had a dream which had any special significance?

6   Science and technology are much more part of our everyday life than when these writers lived. But do we still fear that scientists are meddling with things that would be best left alone? Should there be stricter controls over what sort of research is allowed to continue?

VI : A. *Natural monsters. The girl on the right is normal size.*

VII Written Work

Frankenstein

1   Compare II : *g* and II : *h*. What do you think are the main differences about the way in which the incidents are described?

2   Compare what Mary Shelley says about the effect her story should have (II : 3) with this speech by the character Lord Byron in the foreword to *The Bride of Frankenstein*: "Well, whatever your purpose may have been, my dear, I myself take great relish in savouring each separate horror. I roll them," he said, with unctuous relish, "over my tongue." Now look at Montague Summers's description of vampires (IV : 1). Can you draw any conclusions about different attitudes to horror?

3   The quotation from Milton which appears on the title page of the first edition of *Frankenstein* (VII : A) is often omitted from later editions. Write a new story, using this same quotation as its theme.

4   Write a new story in which the creature Frankenstein brings to life, instead of looking hideous, is physically perfectly beautiful. How would people's reactions differ?

5   The image of the monster which is so popular is both simple and striking. Yet Mary Shelley's monster was a complex and subtle figure. Compare the literary and visual material in chapter II. Is it just the use of words which increases the complexity?

Dr Jekyll and Mr Hyde

1   Which of the pictures of Mr Hyde reproduced in this book comes closest to how you think he should look? Write a detailed description of Hyde, as you think he should be.

2   Look again at VI : JEKYLL AND HYDE 1, the first question in the Discussions section. Take any one of the situations suggested there and write a description of what happens, first when you are accompanied by the character of your choice and secondly when you are accompanied by the other. Invent another new situation of your own.

3   Stevenson said that the subject of *Jekyll and Hyde* is: "that strong sense of man's double nature which must at times come in upon and overwhelm the mind of every thinking creature." Either explain fully what you think he means by that statement or else write another story on the same theme.

4   Dr Lanyon, in his letter to Mr Utterson (III : *c*), talks about his feeling towards Mr Hyde as "disgustful curiosity". Later in the same extract Hyde asks Dr Lanyon: "Has the greed of curiosity too much command of you?" It is curiosity which has led men to

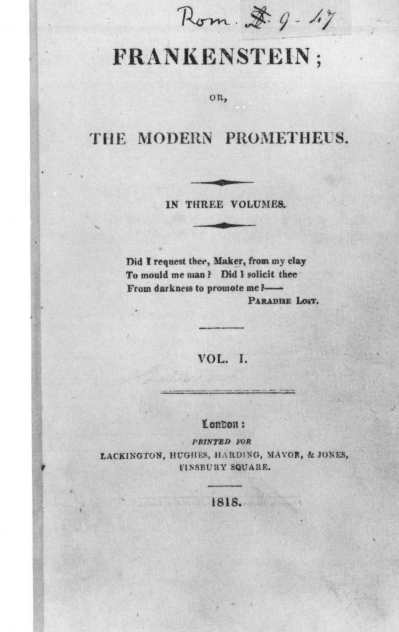

Rom. £ 9 - 17

FRANKENSTEIN;

OR,

THE MODERN PROMETHEUS.

IN THREE VOLUMES.

Did I request thee, Maker, from my clay
To mould me man ? Did I solicit thee
From darkness to promote me ?——
              PARADISE LOST.

VOL. I.

London:
PRINTED FOR
LACKINGTON, HUGHES, HARDING, MAVOR, & JONES,
FINSBURY SQUARE.

1818.

VII : A. *Title page of the first edition of* Frankenstein.

make some of the greatest discoveries in history but it is also curiosity which can lead one into greatest danger. Write about curiosity and what it means to you.

5   We know that Henry Jekyll wrote a last letter to Mr Utterson. Suppose that Edward Hyde had done the same. Write that letter.

Dracula

1   Although the character of Dracula is still alive and well and living in Transylvania, many people find Bram Stoker's book almost unreadable because, they say, his style is so wordy and overdone. From the extracts printed, do you agree with this? Is there any other style which would be better suited to writing about Dracula? Try it.

2   Read again Dreyer's comments (IV : 13). The situation he describes could just as easily be a comedy. Try writing a short comic play on this theme.

3   James Dickie, who has collected a number of vampire stories into a book called *The Undead*, describes the vampire in his introduction as "the hyphen between life and death". What do you think this phrase means? Is it true?

4   Write a story about a working-class vampire.

5   Why do you think there are so few stories in which a vampire attacks a victim of the same sex? Try writing a story in which the vampire, who can be either male or female, prefers victims of the same sex. The story can be frightening or funny, or both.

6   Read this statement by Van Helsing on the nature of belief.

"You are clever man, friend John; you reason well, and your wit is bold; but you are too prejudiced. You do not let your eyes see nor your ears hear, and that which is outside your daily life is not of account to you. Do you not think that there are things which you cannot understand, and yet which are; that some people see things that others cannot? But there are things old and new which must not be contemplate by men's eyes, because they know – or think they know – some things which other men have told them. Ah, it is the fault of our science that it wants to explain all; and if it explain not, then it says there is nothing to explain. But yet we see around us every day the growth of new beliefs, which think themselves new; and which are yet but the old, which pretend to be young – like the fine ladies at the opera. I suppose now you do not believe in corporeal transference. No? Nor in materialization. No? Nor in astral bodies. No? Nor in the reading of thought. No? Nor in hypnotism —"

"Yes," I said. "Charcot has proved that pretty well." He smiled as he went on: "Then you are satisfied as to it. Yes? And of course then you understand how it act, and can follow the mind of the great Charcot – alas that he is no more! – into the very soul of the patient that he influence. No? Then, friend John, am I to take it that you simply accept fact, and are satisfied to let from premise to conclusion be a blank? No? Then tell me – for I am student of the brain – how you accept the hypnotism and reject the thought-reading. Let me tell you, my friend, that there are things done to-day in electrical science which would have been deemed unholy by the very men who discovered electricity – who would themselves not so long before have been burned as wizards. There are always mysteries in life. Why was it that Methuselah lived nine hundred years, and 'Old Parr' one hundred and sixty-nine, and yet that poor Lucy, with four men's blood in her poor veins, could not live even one day! For, had she live one more day, we could have save her. Do you know all the mystery of life and death? Do you know the altogether of comparative anatomy, and can say wherefore the qualities of brutes are in some men, and not in others? Can you tell me why, when other spiders die small and soon, that one great spider lived for centuries in the tower of the old Spanish church and grew and grew, till, on descending, he could drink the oil of all the church lamps? Can you tell me why the Pampas, ay and elsewhere, there are bats that come at night and open the veins of cattle and horses and suck dry their veins; how in some islands of the Western seas there are bats which hang on the trees all day, that those who have seen describe as like giant nuts or pods, and that when the sailors sleep on the deck, because that it is hot, flit down on them, and then – and then in the morning are found dead men, white as even Miss Lucy was?"

"Good God, Professor!" I said, starting up. "Do you mean to tell me that Lucy was bitten by such a bat; and that such a thing is here in London in the nineteenth century?" He waved his hand for silence, and went on: –

"Can you tell me why the tortoise lives more long than generations of men; why the elephant goes on and on till he has seen dynasties; and why the parrot never die only of bite of cat or dog or other complaint? Can you tell me why men believe in all ages and places that there are some few who live on always if they be permit; that there are men and women who cannot die? We all know – because science has vouched for the fact – that there have been toads shut up in rocks for thousands of years, shut in one so small hole that only hold him since the youth of the world. Can you tell me how the Indian fakir can make himself to die and have been buried, and his grave sealed and corn sowed on it, and the corn reaped and be cut and sown and reaped and cut again, and then men come and take away the unbroken seal, and that there lie the Indian fakir, not dead, but that rise up and walk amongst them as before?" Here I interrupted him. I was getting bewildered; he so crowded on my mind his list of nature's eccentricities and possible impossibilities that my imagination was getting fired. I had a dim idea that he was teaching me some lesson, as long ago he used to do in his study at Amsterdam; but he used then to tell me the thing, so that I could have the object of thought in mind all the time. But now I was without his help, yet I wanted to follow him, so I said:

"Professor, let me be your pet student again. Tell me the thesis, so that I may apply your knowledge as you go on. At present I am going in my mind from point to point as a mad man, and not a sane one, follows an idea. I feel like a novice blundering through a bog in a mist, jumping from one tussock to another in the mere blind effort to move on without knowing where I am going."

"That is good image," he said. "Well, I shall tell you. My thesis is this: I want you to believe."

"To believe what?"

"To believe in things that you cannot."

Could you write a reply to this, refuting his argument?

General

1   All three stories, as we have seen, had their origins in dreams. When you waken up tomorrow, write down *immediately* any fragments of dream you remember. Later, see if you can use any of what you have remembered to write a story of any kind at all.

2   None of the three stories we have looked at is a straight narrative. *Frankenstein*, although mostly spoken by Frankenstein himself, is set within the sea captain's voyage of discovery. More than a third of *Dr Jekyll and Mr Hyde* is in the form of letters to Mr Utterson, and *Dracula* (see IV : 8) is written from a number of different points of view. Can you account for this stylistic complexity?

3   Write a new modern myth.

4   Explain your success or lack of success in answering the previous question satisfactorily.

VIII Projects

Frankenstein

1   *Observation*: If you had just been created, what are the things about our everyday environment which would most impress you? Use drawings or still photographs to illustrate.
2   *Research*: Mary Shelley's book is subtitled *The Modern Prometheus*. Find out all you can about the original Prometheus. What parallels really exist between him and Frankenstein?
3   *Survey*: Ask as many people as possible who they think Frankenstein is. See how many assume it is the name of the monster. Ask them where they learned the information. Ask everybody to describe (*a*) the monster and (*b*) what happens in the story. See how many of the descriptions are clearly of Boris Karloff. Try to plot the main variations which people make in the story. It would be interesting to see whether people from the same group (i.e. sex, age, occupation) tended to think the same things.
4   *Drama*: Construct a situation in which you discover by chance that you are a test-tube baby. Improvise the conversation when you confront your parents on the subject.

Dr Jekyll and Mr Hyde

1   *Graphics*: Look at the political cartoon by Garland (VIII : A) which is from the *New Statesman* of 5 January 1973. It uses the idea of Jekyll and Hyde to make a comment on President Nixon's attitude to the halt of bombing in Vietnam. Are there other political or social issues where the idea of Jekyll and Hyde could be used to make a satirical or just a humorous comment? Why is it a particularly good image for use in the sphere of politics and public life? See if you can draw more cartoons using the same basic idea, or a modification of it.
2   *Research*: I explained (III : 6) how Stevenson modelled his character of Jekyll and Hyde to some extent on Deacon Brodie of Edinburgh. Deacon Brodie is a very interesting character in his own right. See how much you can find out about him and his double life.
3   *Survey*: Most people know the names of Jekyll and Hyde. Find out how many people know which is which. Ask them which one they would rather be, and why? How are you going to assess whether they are telling you the truth?
4   *Behaviour*: We all have different ways of behaving at different times. You behave differently at home to how you behave at school. You behave differently with your friends to how you

MR HYDE . . .   . . . AND . . .   . . . DR JEKYLL

VIII : A. *Cartoon from the* New Statesman.

behave at an important interview. These are ways in which we all show a certain amount of willingness to split our personalities. To see how strong the differences between your ways of behaviour are, try changing the way you behave in one set of circumstances to how you normally behave in a quite different set. Behave towards your friends as if they were your aunts and uncles, or as if they were all five years younger than you. If your teacher is a man, behave towards him as if he were a woman, and vice versa. When you go home, behave towards your parents as if you were a paying guest in the house. You will probably find that these experiments quickly cause rows and violent arguments, especially if the people do not know why it is you are behaving differently. See if you can work out the reason for these arguments. Do we all expect people to behave just in the way we like? Are we living in a world full of schizophrenics?

Dracula

1   *Research*: Is there any real evidence to prove that vampires exist? Try to find out any facts which would support people's belief.

2   *Research*: If you have access to a library which keeps files of old newspapers, look up the case of John George Haigh (sentenced to death 9 July 1949, hanged 15 August 1949) and see if you can come to any conclusions about the kind of man he was. Do you think he was mad or not? Should he have been hanged?

3   *Survey*: Most practical joke shops sell sets of "Dracula fangs". Buy a set, practise talking with them in your mouth and, when you are able to keep them in easily, try conducting a survey on

vampirism. Ask people a series of questions on whether they believe in vampires and what exactly they think vampires can and can not do. The results will, in any case, be valuable. See how long it takes them to notice your fangs and what their reactions are. If any of them appear either frightened or angry, follow up with a more searching interview about their general belief in the supernatural.

4   *Drama*: It is the middle of the night. You have come in late from a party. You decide to have a bath. You have been happily washing your feet when suddenly you look up to find Dracula crouching beside your bath, fangs bared, ready to plunge them into your soft neck. You have no garlic or crucifix to hand, so your only hope is to stall him until dawn. Try to improvise a conversation where the victim tries to keep the vampire talking until daybreak.

General

1   *Drama*: Let the characters meet. Improvise a confrontation between Frankenstein and his monster, Dr Jekyll and Mr Hyde (both together as separate people) and Dracula. This can either take the form of a static interview in which each tries to assert his own importance as *the* modern myth, or else you can improvise some bizarre and unlikely story involving all these char-

2   *Drama and Graphics*: Apart from goods directly related to the horror industry itself (like masks, models and blow-up monsters) can you think of other ways commercial enterprises could use the material in these modern myths? Try setting up a group of people as an advertising agency to see what sort of campaigns you could run on these lines. For example, in Birmingham the Blood Transfusion Service ran a publicity campaign to coincide with the release of Terence Fisher's Hammer version of *Dracula*. What about *Frankenstein* for the Central Electricity Generating Board or *Jekyll and Hyde* for a patent drug company? Is it possible that this kind of campaign would actually discourage people from using a product rather than encouraging them?

IX Film Making

1   This section is about the general lines that film-making in this sort of subject can take. Because of the more complex nature of the techniques involved, I have not included such specific questions as in the other areas of work. There are suggestions for various methods of approach but in group projects of this kind, it is usually best if the whole process from first idea through scripting to final cut comes from the group itself rather than being imposed from outside. Of course, not everybody has available the facilities of using film (8 mm or 16 mm) or VTR equipment. Some of the ideas suggested in this section could, however, be adapted for sound only and could be produced as an edited tape. The section is designed, nevertheless, primarily for those who do have access to film equipment of some kind.

2   It is very easy to make bad horror movies. It is not very impressive. If you try to compete with the Hollywood and Hammer epics in their own terms, you are almost certain to come off as rather poor imitations. Even the professionals, with whole studios and tens of thousands of dollars at their disposal for each scene, do not always succeed in making their films convincing. Particularly since, if you choose to concentrate on *Frankenstein*, *Dr Jekyll and Mr Hyde* or *Dracula*, there are already established film images which people are used to and with which you would have to compete, it is broadly speaking a bad idea simply to try to remake the commercial films. It is also more original and more interesting to try to rethink the whole idea from the outset.

3   There are two main lines your film-making can take. The first is to make a parody. Although this has already been tried in all three cases, there is still plenty of scope for alternative versions. In the case of *Frankenstein*, the parody has taken the form of *The Munsters* television series, which was broadcast in the 60s and was based on Charles Addams cartoons. If you look at Illustration IX : A you can see that the idea is to parody the more sensational aspects of the story by making them seem quite normal or commonplace. *Jekyll and Hyde*, as I mentioned in III : 16, has already been parodied by Jerry Lewis, but the possibilities for situation comedy, especially if you keep the heroines, are really endless, given the kind of confusion that might occur when one man can change his identity, either at will or when he does not expect it. As for *Dracula*, Roman Polanski's *Dance of the Vampires* is probably the funniest film on the subject. Certainly, the whole vampire legend can easily be manipulated so that the whole thing seems quite ridiculous. Remember, in all these cases, that suspense, which is so important an aspect of

IX:A. *One of Charles Addams'*
black humour cartoons. Drawing by
Chas. Addams; Copr. 1938, 1966
The New Yorker Magazine, Inc.

"Oh, it's you! For a moment you gave me quite a start."

IX : B. *An extract from the horror comic* Mystery Tales *no 17.*

horror, is also an integral part of comedy. It is simply used to different ends.

4   One easy way to achieve a new and amusing view of a story is to change its setting. The story of *Frankenstein* would seem very different set in a school chemistry lab. It is also possible to make imitation early silent movies by filming in black and white and running your camera slightly slower than usual. This has the added advantage of requiring no soundtrack.

5   The other main line which your film-making can take is to rethink the story quite seriously but in modern and more immediately relevant terms. For *Frankenstein* you could concentrate on the idea of spare-part surgery, which is very topical and which could be treated from several different points of view. Any modern version of *Jekyll and Hyde* would be most liable to concentrate on the schizophrenic view of the character. An interesting case-history of a person with a split personality could be developed in cinematic terms, perhaps using a semi-documentary style. If *Dracula* was simply put into a modern middle-class context, it could be made to seem even more threatening; or you could choose to concentrate on a particular aspect of the vampire legend, such as cannibalism or the death wish.

6   You could explore the whole area of the relationship between the illusion of these myths and their possible terrifying reality. Just as the comic strip of Dracula (IX : B) does, you could create situations in which a comfortable illusion suddenly achieves startling reality. This is an interesting theme for a film because it is dealing with why these stories have their special kind of hold over us.

7   The point about all these suggestions is that they can be technically as simple or as complex as you have time and equipment to make them. They could all be made with or without synchronized sound, for example, and their length would depend on how far you developed the idea into a story. The possibilities are endless. Remember that it is not necessary to be scientifically or literally accurate. What matters is rather to *seem* authentic, by whatever means you like.

List of Illustrations